Cambridge Elements

Elements in Histories of Emotions and the Senses

edited by
Rob Boddice
Tampere University
Piroska Nagy
Université du Québec à Montréal (UQAM)
Mark Smith
University of South Carolina

DISENCHANTING THE SENSES

Sulfuric Discourse and the World System

Andrew Kettler
University of South Carolina

CAMBRIDGE
UNIVERSITY PRESS

Shaftesbury Road, Cambridge CB2 8EA, United Kingdom

One Liberty Plaza, 20th Floor, New York, NY 10006, USA

477 Williamstown Road, Port Melbourne, VIC 3207, Australia

314–321, 3rd Floor, Plot 3, Splendor Forum, Jasola District Centre,
New Delhi – 110025, India

103 Penang Road, #05–06/07, Visioncrest Commercial, Singapore 238467

Cambridge University Press is part of Cambridge University Press & Assessment,
a department of the University of Cambridge.

We share the University's mission to contribute to society through the pursuit of
education, learning and research at the highest international levels of excellence.

www.cambridge.org
Information on this title: www.cambridge.org/9781009532952

DOI: 10.1017/9781009446938

© Andrew Kettler 2025

This publication is in copyright. Subject to statutory exception and to the provisions
of relevant collective licensing agreements, no reproduction of any part may take
place without the written permission of Cambridge University Press & Assessment.

When citing this work, please include a reference to the DOI 10.1017/9781009446938

First published 2025

A catalogue record for this publication is available from the British Library

ISBN 978-1-009-53295-2 Hardback
ISBN 978-1-009-44694-5 Paperback
ISSN 2632-1068 (online)
ISSN 2632-105X (print)

Cambridge University Press & Assessment has no responsibility for the persistence
or accuracy of URLs for external or third-party internet websites referred to in this
publication and does not guarantee that any content on such websites is, or will remain,
accurate or appropriate.

For EU product safety concerns, contact us at Calle de José Abascal, 56, 1°, 28003
Madrid, Spain, or email eugpsr@cambridge.org

Disenchanting the Senses

Sulfuric Discourse and the World System

Elements in Histories of Emotions and the Senses

DOI: 10.1017/9781009446938
First published online: November 2025

Andrew Kettler
University of South Carolina

Author for correspondence: Andrew Kettler, kettlera@email.sc.edu

Abstract: Specifically standing between humanity and natural perceptions of the environment in the contemporary age of ecological decay are disenchanted meanings of sulfur and evil that changed to support the base of capitalism during the Early Modern Era. The blinding system of linguistic and material networks that capital constructs to deny humans the ability to sense environmental threat can be understood most notably through a history of ideas related to supposedly sulfuric demons and the discursive archaeology surrounding many toxic sulfuric compounds ardently linked with the Anthropocene. Thinking of cause and effect in networks of objects and humans, as well as the structures of modernity and capitalism, this Element reasserts a philosophy of disenchantment into the history of the environment. At the core of modernity, capitalist discourses greenwashed experiences of the body related to evils of environmental threat to protect the means of production from considerable critique during the Industrial Revolution.

This Element also has a video abstract:
www.cambridge.org/HOES_Kettler_abstract

Keywords: Disenchantment, sulfur, sensation, demons, coal

ISBNs: 9781009532952 (HB), 9781009446945 (PB), 9781009446938 (OC)
ISSNs: 2632-1068 (online), 2632-105X (print)

Contents

1 Sulfur, Sensation, and Modernity   1

2 Sensing the Devil in the Early Modern Era   15

3 Sulfur, Othering, and Early Modern Empires   22

4 The Devil's Demise   31

5 Brimstone Frontiers   37

6 Sulfur Shifted, Sulfur Contained   47

References   56

1 Sulfur, Sensation, and Modernity

Capital hides its sins. Rather than solely attempt to obscure material sins, which often leak out from landfills, toxic waste dumps, and other uncovered spaces of even greater malfeasance that forces plastic into the cells of the human body, capital has also learned to conceal profitable depravities in more profound manners. Through attempting to manipulate human perception through the power of language, capital hides its greatest crimes from the masses who would otherwise be able to detect malfeasance. Through systems of language, capital alters sensory worlds to conceal the violence that it emplaces upon the earth. Educating bodies how to better sense the pollution, in a battle against the bourgeoisie who work to desensitize humans from sensing ecological decline, must accordingly become a hallmark of future praxis, as capital breeds percepticide to prevent the sensing body from becoming a revolutionary force that detects the sins of profit and then acts on that vital detection.

Networks of words, objects, and bodies link in vast connections that manifest how human beings come to understand perceptual reality of diverse ecologies. The interactions between objects, bodies, and ideological forces produce perceptions of socially constructed reality through webs of signs that generate patterns of understanding leading to a common acceptance of what exists in the world through agreement between the self and diverse others (Latour 2007; Derrida 2011; Pennartz 2024; Toadvine 2024, 201–234). Specifically standing between humanity and the perception of nature in the contemporary age of decay are superstructural meanings produced to support the base of capitalism. There were, no doubt, significant material changes throughout the Early Modern Era that also worked to make the world less sensorially intense in general, as with sewage improvements explored by scholars in the wake of seminal work on the topic from Alain Corbin (1986). Coinciding with the desensitization cause by a less odorific world, capital often also breeds forms of percepticide, the cultivated death of any remnant natural perception, to promote the fetishization of all things so all objects and beings can be consumed as commodified products. As this fetishization occurs materially, the system also works through the power of language to hide profitable sins by ruining the human ability to perceive ecological threat through the sensorium. Such percepticide, as a historical philosophy, arises from the oppressions of Latin American dictatorships and the conservative ability to manipulate resources, through fear of scarcity and more subtle means, to promote the power of specifically interested political forces (Taylor 2020, Masiello 2018).

Capital desires that humanity forget the air is becoming unbreathable. Humans generally follow their call and disregard the need to purposefully sense the air, continuing to understand breathing as a passive action. Forms of modern phenomenology contrastingly suggest that humanity must come to a greater understanding that the air is a space much more prone to ingenuity than the earth, as a space where the body lives in an atmosphere ripe with pickings of any range of emotional, affective, and sensory possibilities. The earth grounds us, the air lifts us up into hopeful states that can allow for utopian imaginings of the senses that conservative and corporate interests interested only in the blood and land can never truly grasp or imagine. As Luce Irigaray noted in her analysis of the false grounding of the earth and the disregarding of the air in the works of Martin Heidegger, "In forgetting the air that is breathed, the air that is occupied, forgetting the livable place where the being man appears and is encountered-these forgettings together become the possibility for remembering a nonexistent permanence. A being-there" (Irigaray 1999, 164).

Rather than being-there in the supposed permanence of the earth with Heidegger and his noxious allies, humans should choose to live and think within the impermanent atmosphere, and must protect that space from the wealthy, fascist, and gerontocratic fossil fuel abusers of the modern world who continue to forget the air through polluting the atmosphere at their will. The forces that protect polluters and abuse the concept of truth that is needed to critique that exploitation can increase, as Irigaray points out, into stages that push to the brink of fascism that protects the land, and its pollutants, as a way to defend the idea of the nation through violent resistance. As Karl Steel proposes in a reading of the phenomenology of Irigaray's critique of Heidegger through the works of Emmanuel Levinas,

> Air enables thought, more vitally than Heidegger's earth, for without more air than earth, there could be no clearing that could make thought possible . . . We share our breathing with others through our incarnational being here; air reminds us that in being here together we also share an inescapable condition of shared vulnerability . . . Barring the otherwise unconsidered needs of anaerobic bacteria, without air, there is no thought, no being, no life. (Steel 2015, 211–212)[1]

Thinking through such phenomenological ponderings on the importance of the air allows a reading of the world system that focuses on diverse perceptions of sulfuric atmospheres. The world system emerged to its modern prominent network through linking cores and peripheries in a grand mélange of profit for the bourgeoisie through material exchanges, the material work of abused laborers, and the material infrastructure of mines and factories. As well, the world system developed through discursive manipulation, the marking of a new

---

[1] See also the reading of modern literature and breathing within Heine (2021).

order of things that supported the economic base of core and periphery relations through justifications that delimited peripheral colonized persons as sensorially different and inferior to those in Western metropoles. That problematic discursive manipulation continues today, as Indigenous bodies and minds are still believed unable to grasp environmental issues through the supposedly more practical manners of the Western capitalist who is deemed better to judge risk, sacrifice, and scarcity to balance the needs of the fossil fuel present against the possible futures of the earth and market (Haraway 2016; Clary-Lemon 2019).

In the coming age of mass automation in the planetary mine of arriving Artificial Intelligence, it will become increasingly important to link the ability of human bodies to perceive the threats that capital hopes to hide from the senses of subalterns. The masses must notice such manipulations, as with the absurdity of "clean coal" in a discursive sense, and attempt to pursue decarbonization and degrowth to provide any chance for the world to survive with humans as a considerable part of the global economic system. Capital desires such automation of the planetary mine as an ultimate step in even greater percepticide, with the desire to possibly kill the human body that stands in the way of greater profit, as capitalism could simply function without humans, or completely alter the human form, if the human body stands too much in the way of the continued growth of future dividends (Bostrom 2014; Frase 2016, 120–143; Arboleda 2020; Saltmarsh 2021, 12–29).[2]

In such a space of technological acceleration and failing human resistance, it becomes vital for ecological activists to promote the cultivation of sensory skills with a knowledge that discourse often works to manipulate human sensation for the aims of the bourgeoisie, human or nonhuman, as a way to maintain the controls of the moneyed upon the means of production. Percepticide could not, in the past few centuries, complete the erasure of the ecological sins that the body continues to skillfully sense because many individuals maintained the ability, through persistent somatic work, to sense the world beyond the manners that capital wanted them to recognize. Sensory skills are those culturally educated perceptual talents that are judged with greater value in a specific society, and those in that culture gain cultural capital from cultivating those ways of sensing the world. Nearly all sensory skills are informed, altered, and constructed within cultural dialogue with hegemonic influences that provide understandings of how to perceive the world, as studied within the anthropology of Marcel Mauss and through the articulation of diverse techniques of the senses from David Howes (Mauss 1973, 70–88; Howes 1991, 182–184). Numerous other scholars have discussed the importance of sensory skills in diverse

---

[2] For more on degrowth see Soper (2023); Saito (2024).

contexts away from such hegemonic influences, from Western theory on the history of the body through phenomenology and often upon sensory worlds apart from the Western that do not include the stained sensorium of those bodies most invaded by capital (Jenner 2010; Reinarz 2012). These personal and cultural negotiations concerning how to sense the world often enter the body and mind in uncanny manners, involving what Jacques Rancière has articulated through understanding the "distribution of the sensible," Davide Panagia has discussed through political influences of power upon sensation, and Constance Classen has provided in readings of "Other Ways to Wisdom" (Classen 1999; Rancière 2004, 32–50; Panagia 2010).

Joy Parr has specifically portrayed how institutions often work to alter the influence of sensory skills to cultivate an inability of the modern body to sense the changes happening to the perceptual apparatuses in specific environments, disrupting embodied understandings of how the environment functioned in a past unburdened by the chemical and capitalist invasions of the twentieth century. For example, in diverse Canadian laboring environments, sulfur dioxide and hydrogen sulfide can become so prominent as to reach parts per million (ppm) so extraordinary as to materially destroy olfactory cells, as many workers came to understand, when working in specific industrial settings, that the greatest threat arises not when smelling sulfur, but when the ability to smell the toxicity stops and the vertigo begins (Parr 2010, 141–160). Capital does not need to be abusive upon human sensation, in different historical moments it has been less controlling than others, but in recent decades since the rise of neoliberalism the manipulation of human sensation has accelerated to increasingly unfelt places. Human subjects may be able to perceive the world in dialogue with the sensory influences that economic systems emplace upon the body, but modern populations can never fully escape efforts to alter and degrade the sensorium (Ingold 2011, 214–226).

Within these capitalist influences on sensation and desensitization, transitions between energy regimes have frequently involved making bodies able to subsist both biologically and culturally next to corruptive materials. These discursive conversions occurring during changes to energy regimes, as with the consequential biomass to coal transition of the Industrial Revolution, are frequently culturally debated during their historical moments (Stradling 1999; Melosi 2008; Wrigley 2010, Smil 2016, Kiechle 2017; Gross and Needham 2023). However, those debates on shifting energies and the rise of sulfuric atmospheres seldom engage how the body was also being produced by powerful discourses and incentives to experience the world in the accelerating manners that the newly arriving energy regime desired those bodies to feel and experience, as we often know much less about the environment and its effects upon bodies than what is generally accepted in the public sphere (Prager 2020, 71–97).[3]

Through embodied manipulations of the body within language and media, capital valorizes production and profit, especially above the rights of the human body to not suffer, which can cause that physical form to frequently become detritus to the economic system if it inhibits the expansion of value. In many ways, current forms of capital push against an earth that cannot sustain its wishes for more profit. A rift develops between the economic system that wants greater production and a natural world, and human bodies, that cannot handle accelerated forms of pollution and sulfuric toxicity (Mészáros 2010; Tsing 2017, 58–70). Rather than understand these rifts between the dominant economic system and the future of humanity, what becomes more common in the discourse on climate change and global warming is an acceptance of shared responsibility of all and a lessening of responsibility on the true makers of modern crisis, the means of production scarring the earth to push beyond the limits of worldly profits, a push that may soon make the gesture to move beyond the human that exists as an increasing limitation to expanding value (Malm 2016; Farrier 2019; Chakrabarty 2023) (Figure 1).

Responsibility is increasingly displaced from the guilty owners in the modern world, those bathing knee-deep in the slick profits of the Tar Sands, and is currently placed upon common people who must use fossil fuels at the base of the economy to survive. The great acceleration of climate change is a product of class warfare through these material and linguistic manipulations. As Nicholas Paliewicz provides in his analysis of Rio Tinto, a multinational mining conglomerate, corporate entities work in both core and peripheral settings to purposefully alter meanings of environmental protection. The corporate persona emerges in these spaces as a figure who can displace any act that may be considered violating of the environment or abusive of local populations into networks of corporate language because those persons and corporations have no long-term interest in the regions that are mined (Paliewicz 2024). Rather than something that can be solved with personal choices to use less, climate change must consequently be addressed in a structural manner with plans through the proletariat against the bourgeoisie, because global warming is mostly arriving from the choices of the extremely wealthy to use the environment. The only way out of the continuing heating involves a working-class solidarity that understands vast ecological threats through newly cultivated sensory skills that can be used to build a resistance that finds in rising against the means of production an ability to also overcome percepticide (Moore 2015; Huber 2022, 283–296).

---

[3] See also energy transitions in a comparative analysis within Vergara (2021, 221–226).

Figure 1 Charles Sheeler's *Classic Landscape* (1931) portrays the links between industry the civilizing process in American art and culture. In this exceedingly clean portrayal of Ford Motor Company's River Rouge Plant near Detroit, Sheeler offers modern American industry as akin to classical Greek and Roman architecture. The plant, the largest in the world at the time, produced automotives for the burgeoning American economy produced upon Henry Ford's assembly line. Capitalism often valorizes through narratives linking the economic system to assertions of cultural progress, portraying its cleanliness as part of a civilization that has solely provided greatness to the world. Charles Sheeler, *Classic Landscape* (1931), National Gallery of Art. Public Domain.

Energy regime changes, which in modern history have instituted accelerations of fossil fuels over animal labor and organic fuels, also contribute vast feedback loops into the social fabric of influential networks of meaning and sensing and are consequently understood in their present moments by those who feel the changes upon their bodies and their societies, whether through uncanny affect or through more definitive understandings of sensory change. The state, the means of production, and the public sphere manifest diverse aesthetics of control through narratives of valorization that are meant to seep into the social fabric and alter embodied experiences of the world (Crary 1990; Eagleton 1990; Redfield 2003, 176–182). This Element asks, to what extent did historical people succumb to these material and linguistic changes during increases in sulfuric toxicity? As E.A. Wrigley has summarized in the case of fossil fuels and modernity in these contexts,

> The nature of the Industrial Revolution meant that its completion, rather than heralding a reduction in further change, often entailed the opposite. When, and only when, both heat and mechanical energy could be secured without apparent limit in all locations and with much-reduced regional price variations, was it possible for exponential growth to become the norm, but completion of an industrial revolution proved to imply continued change rather than a new stability.

Under these regime changes of the modern age, capital valorizes energy as solving the problem of scarcity and heralding in a new sense of permanency, while at the same time inventing new forms of scarcity to justify the expenditure of more energy to create ever more chaos and change (Wrigley 2016, 198–205, 205; Crockett 2022, 132–184).

As Tad Delay also proposes, "a legal and political superstructure built atop the particular exploitations unique to fossil fuels will react violently in concert when its base is threatened" (2024, 206). The superstructure that justifies the profits of the base that is reliant upon fossil fuel energy and these constantly evolving narratives of valorization knows the risk that human resistance to pollution causes to the continued growth of value, and consequently attempts to alter bodies to not sense the environmental threats that are created in the drive for profit. These narratives that influence minds and bodies involve valorization of capital that also circulates descriptions that assert rejection of any data that shows the negative impacts of capital upon the climate. These superstructures with fossil fuels at the base are also vital in the creation of diverse siege mentalities involving national and local identities that work to retain profit, as explored by Andrea Marston for Bolivian plurinational mining operations (2024).

In the eighteenth century, fossil fuels began to completely divorce capital from the natural world of seasonal agriculture, as the ordinary flows of rivers and weather patterns became less of a threat to the standardization of value and growth. Economic movement forward and the use of the discursive power of scarcity created diverse bourgeois narrative influences during the era of primitive accumulation as the dominance over coal supplies and commodity networks kept individuals alive in harsh winters and was valorized alongside the power of the nation-state (Boyer 2023, 11–44). For Andreas Malm, the bourgeoisie specifically gained such manipulative power over the economic base due to coal at the primary moments of accumulation and maintains that early dominance through extraction with the current control on energy regimes that accept even greater mass automation. Steam engines, or "puffing devils" in the parlance of the time of their creation, did not tire as human labor, and the bourgeois found in the increased use of machinery an ability to suppress labor resistance through pitting inexhaustible machines against the human body, which frequently had to face days of 100 degrees labor next to coal furnaces, the pits of deathly mines, and rickets caused by blacked-out sun when coal and sulfuric lifeways became quotidian (2016, 194–222).

Capitalism was also valorized through the innovators of these heroic machines that rose as essential above any concern with protecting labor, as those machines linked with the progress of nationalism and a strong masculine identity that would overcome any threat of scarcity. Accelerating into forms of modern energy fascism, present forms of neoliberal and disaster capitalism link the fear of racist intrusion and the still prominent promotion of whiteness with the desire to continue domination of the land and sky. Blood and land, that old fascist moniker, rises with far-right modern linkages to major fossil fuel corporations, coal and gas forms of nationalism and austerity, machine labor driven by fuel from the earth, and the idea that moving away from modern energy regimes is feminine and a threat to civilization (Alaimo 2016, 91–110; Dagget 2019; Malm 2021, 315–398).

Sulfuric excess, breathing sulfuric air, and other compounding toxic existences are all justified through constructed narratives that valorize capitalism as the only natural economic system. Sulfur was essential alongside applied metals and extractive processes in the first world system based on peripheral extraction from the Global South after the discovery of the New World during the Early Modern Era. Based in theft of resources from the periphery, and specific incorporation of intelligences related to metals from the Near East and China, the West accelerated and accumulated primitive accumulations of value from the hands of global others. As Jack Goody has shown, smelting knowledge, recipes for gunpowder, and metalworking came from the East and was solidified and accelerated in the West due to manufacturers incentivized by a new economic system of capital and due to the abundance of coal, sulfur, timber, and iron throughout European spaces of the Early Modern Era and into the Victorian Age (2012, 285–300; Fors 2015). Specifically, gunpowder not only arrived in its tripartite and combined physical form from the East, but its arrival to Europe included initial recipes for its construction as five parts saltpeter, two parts sulfur, and one part carbon. Gunpowder, "made from charcoal, sulfur, and saltpeter, burns upon ignition, propagating a spray of molten salts between its grains, and releases gas in the form of smoke." Early modern battlefields smelled of sulfur due to this recipe of Eastern extraction that hit the European continent in the fourteenth century with considerable force and became common in the militaries of the fifteenth century and onward into the age of the New Model Army and settler colonialist warfare throughout the supposedly savage spaces of the colonial world (Brugh 2019, 94–97, 94).

As Lowell Duckert displays through a reading of John Milton's *Paradise Lost* (1666) that engages with material history of products like coal and gunpowder, religious myth can allow for a greater understanding of ecological awareness and the modern crisis of the Anthropocene. Such a reading also can link myth to medicine and ecology as histories of the black death, and the "carbuncles" and dark swelling of the nodes due to the disease, came from the Latin "Carbunculus" meaning "small coal" or "Charcoal" common in use during the High Middle Ages. Coal airs had begun to rise around 1268 in England, with the first conflict between merchants and the state on coal rights in Newcastle. By 1285, Edward I banned coal's use, but numerous inventive uses for the rock, especially for creations of pig iron, led to the continuation of its use in legal and illegal eras until the 1570s, when coal burning surged through its prominent use within beer kilns. By 1600, coal became the primary fuel for iron production and heating in England. Due to the rise of coal, Milton was writing during an era of early ecological crisis and framing his reading through the lens of heaven and hell in a time of intense sulfuric airs that rise from coal burning (Duckert 2015, 237–268).

William Rosen also analyzes how sulfuric impurities in steel and iron became vital at the base of modern economic regimes that followed such economic and military introductions and the literary acknowledgments of economic change as sulfur rose from a past of alchemical combinations in the Early Modern Era to become an essential ingredient in major industrial processes of contemporary life. Sulfur rose to even greater importance through the many waves of the Industrial Revolution, especially for the creation of sodium carbonate, essential for manufacturing glass and paper, to produce bleach and fertilizers, in the manufacture of rubber through vulcanization, and in the production of artificial light through recipes for dipped matches. Sulfur became the philosopher's stone of modern capitalism, the alchemical tool that figuratively turned waste into gold. Since the nineteenth century, modern industrialists have often applied statistical measures whereby levels of sulfuric acid produced in a nation function as a basis for understanding the amount of industrial production in that country as sulfuric compounds are so vital to many essential manufacturing processes (2012, 106–108, 148–150).

In the specific production of matches, as Jeremy Zallen has shown, children who worked in American and English matchstick factories of the nineteenth century often glowed and became maimed through the work with sulfuric mixtures of dipped matches, which caused a weakening and breakdown of their jawbones due to nearness to toxic chemical compounds, including the more directly potent phosphorus, which mixed with sulfur to cause their bodies and clothes to smell well after leaving the factory floor (2019, 168–170). The blinding system of linguistic and material networks that capital constructs to deny humans the ability to sense or significantly care about environmental threat to workers, to the extent that children's faces can deconstruct and have their "phossy jaws" fall to the floor in specific histories, can be understood most notably through a history of sulfur and the discursive archaeology surrounding many toxic sulfuric compounds that have been enlisted for profit since the Early Modern Era.

In the past decade, I have published numerous essays that expound on the changes in the perception of sulfur over time through direct work with primary sources related to early modern literature, colonialism, and borderlands (Kettler 2016; Kettler 2020; Kettler 2024). Using expansions on sensory theory and environmental activism this Element builds on those analyses of sulfuric perception to think in more significant terms related to network theory and the human inability to significantly counter the ravages of capital in the Anthropocene through the cultivation of sensory skills, sense work, or citizen-sensing movements. These new theoretical developments further expose that capital uses language to abstract human perceptions away from understanding significant threats, even as ecological movements try to remind the sensing body of newly arriving ecological pressures. The production of ecological percepticide keeps humans from exhibiting any considerable or united praxis against the increasing powers of capital to destroy the earth (Kettler 2022) (Figure 2).

Disenchanting the Senses sets out sensory theory for reading material objects across eras of vast historical time and within the contexts of fossil fuel extraction, industrial residues, and discursive manipulation, whether in the European cores of the Early Modern Era, in the colonial spaces of the abused periphery, or in the later settler colonialist spaces of North America and a twentieth century wastelanded by the American military industrial complex. Thinking of cause and effect in networks of objects and humans, as well as the structures of modernity and capitalism, *Disenchanting the Senses* reasserts a philosophy of disenchantment into the history of the environment. Disenchantment, as a historical concept from roots with the works of Max Weber and most directly articulated by Keith Thomas, can be defined as the Western movement to desacralize knowledge that began during the Renaissance and accelerated through the Reformation, the Enlightenment, and into the age of Positivism. Desacralization implies the shifting of knowledge from that defined by the Church to that defined by natural philosophers and then scientists, many of

Figure 2 Sulfur and sulfuric compounds are directly included in many current industrial and agricultural processes, including steel pickling, rubber vulcanization, and diverse formulas for insecticides and fumigations. The yellow element and its compounds also exist as part of many different byproducts from industrial processes, especially from fossil fuel burning. "Sulfur Dusting of Grape Vines, 5/1972." National Archives. Record Group 412: Records of the Environmental Protection Agency, 1944 – 2006. DOCUMERICA: The Environmental Protection Agency's Program to Photographically Document Subjects of Environmental Concern, 1972–1977. Courtesy of the Library of Congress.

which were in employment of governments or working through entrepreneurial or corporate desire for wealth (Thomas 1971). At the core of modernity, as this Element argues, capitalist discourses greenwashed embodied experiences of the body related to environmental threat to protect the means of production from considerable critique, involving disenchanting processes which continue into an age of intense modern skepticism against the truth of climate change and global warming (Tuan 1974; Haltinner and Sarathchandra 2023; Fressoz 2024).

To tell this tale of disenchantment through the multifarious object of sulfur and its many toxic compounds, Section 2 explores the history of sulfur into the early seventeenth century, studying specific connections between sulfuric understandings of the underworld and hell in European societies, mostly related to English texts and diverse hunts for demons and witches. The second section looks at the links between discourse about demons and the effects of that language upon the experience of bodies in the lived world of supernaturally informed European lifeways. Focusing mostly on witchcraft, the second part of Section 2 offers many examples that connected witches to sulfuric exhalations in the cores of different European nations. Networks of contagion between bodies and miasmic objects of the air created significant fears within these different religious and secular spheres (Camporesi 1994, 15–31; Anderton and Leonard 2004).

Demons have often been employed to better understand scientific worlds, frequently involving the role of imaginary entities in the construction of scientific experimentation, especially in thought experiments related to developing epistemologies. Scholars often raise demons to judge new pathways forward against those demons – as with Artificial Intelligence, a possibly demonic force, to currently be planned against. Miquel Cervantes raised a narrative of demons and knightly insanity to question religious worship, perceptual flaws, and the belief in sulfuric airs linked to demons within *Don Quixote* (1615), specifically when Sancho relays to the errant knight that a supposed demon, the wealthy Don Fernando, is no such demon because the figure smelled of "ambergris from a couple miles away." This essay raises the questions of stinking demons again, to interrogate the inability of modern humans to engage with sensing the evil being done to the environment in the name of profit (Canales 2022, 18–23, 313–324).

Section 3 looks at sulfur in the diverse texts of colonialism, proposing that a central aspect of disenchantment involved shifting stinking witches and demons from the core to the periphery. Colonial discourses about sulfuric demons, especially through Spanish, French, and English writings about the hellishness of subaltern rituals, involved ecological fictions that linked sulfuric metals to racialized bodies. Sulfuric and brimstone atmospheres in the colonized world, whether observed above Native American communities or influencing wayward colonists are but one aspect of the phenomenological shift of malevolent Old World miasmas merging with colonized environments that were fictionalized into what Westerners understood through religious narratives and for the promotion of the colonial project within the mineshafts at the cradle of those developments (Kettler 2022).[4]

I expand on earlier work on this topic through providing that these movements to attribute inferior or evil ways of sensing to Indigenous populations have framed the epistemologies of the Global South throughout the modern world as less able to be trusted to make ecological and economic decisions. Such epistemological dismissal and the acceptance of material violence against

---

[4] For embodiment and geology in the Atlantic World, see Della Dora (2021, 274–278); Mulry (2021, 257–264).

Indigenous bodies through narratives of miasmic evil led to greater Western European justification for their labor acquisitions of Native Americans and other imported workers, as within the gold mines of Hispaniola that triggered greater Spanish intrusion throughout the Western Hemisphere, the mercurial silver flues of northern New Spain and Potosí at the outset of globalization, or deep within the tin mines of Bolivia during the Industrial Revolution, wherein twentieth-century workers often linked the devil of capitalism to the underworld they had to inhabit during their working hours (Nash 1993, 121–169; Testot 2020, 207–225).

Silver mines specifically used sulfur for most of the colonial era and into the industrial era of significant connections to steam power through using zinc sulfide, which was applied to separate silver from ore. The prominence of the mercury-sulfur doctrine and the use of zinc sulfide as a purifier specifically dominated Spanish silver mining discourse during the eighteenth century (Robins 2011, 57–84; Bigelow 2020, 128–131). Such a process was toxic in its initial combination, released poisonous gases into the air breathed by laborers, and became even more noxious into the Anthropocene due to runoff into wells near sulfur mines throughout the Americas, many of which remain as threatening toxic spaces today (Studnicki-Gizbert and Schecter 2010; Johnson 2019; Gomez 2020).

Section 4 of the Element then proposes that the core shifted internally as well, whereby disenchantment in the metropole began through moving the sulfuric connotations of witches and demons from the environments of Western Europe to the periphery, and then a supposedly cleansed core worked to mock previous connotations of sulfuric witches in Europe due to the fresh economic incentives of industrial modernity. The comedic world of sulfur emerged to great force in the literatures of the seventeenth and eighteenth centuries, involving plays, prose, and folklore that questioned the links between the devil and brimstone in creative and comedic manners (Kettler 2024). As I have shown elsewhere, and expand in this Element, fiction, folklore, and narrative about the environment specifically provide ways of understanding how these materials of toxicity were understood in eras prior to chemical understandings of pollution in the twentieth century, a process of narrativizing also articulated in the analysis of the nineteenth-century environment from Jesse Oak Taylor (2016).

Using literatures of the stage and science, Section 4 explores how the core purified through these shifts, whereby the nineteenth century emerged as the most observably sulfuric of eras within Europe, and England proper, due to coal smoke, gunpowder, and sulfuric recipes for greater agricultural production, as the demonic connotations of sulfur were no longer potent for much of the population. The function of the senses changed, a theoretical concept explored by leading phenomenologists in diverse modern historiographical contexts, even as religious belief continued in the minds of early modern practitioners (Merleau-Ponty 1962; Jütte 2005; Schellenberg 2018, 103–113).

Section 5 then shows another shift, whereby the newly cleansed Westerner emerged more forcefully into the colonial world of the nineteenth century without concerns over encountering sulfuric demons in the occupied spaces of empire. When famed archaeologist William Loftus first surveyed the Middle East as part of the Turco-Persian Frontier Commission in 1849, it was the "unbearable stench of sulphur" that signified oil to his senses and to additional travelers to the region (Morton 2017, 16–17). Rather than sense the devil in the products of sulfur on the periphery, colonizers like Loftus in employ of the British crown, and corporate profiteers searching out their own wealth, sensed profit in minerals, sulfur baths, sulfur soaps, rubber, and geological explorations (Kettler 2020). The treatment of sulfuric "flowers" specifically became common in the American South to engage with yellow fever in its supposed miasmic suspension (Olivarius 2022, 104). Sulfur was used to kill rats, fumigate against diseases through eliminating mosquitoes, and produce deathly bleaches and other laundering provisions, becoming a common element in the compounds of everyday life of the early twentieth century, often saving lives while also providing toxicity in a complex exchange of foul and fragrant (Von Hippel 2020).

Sulfuric connotations of evil were rarely considered, in the search for profit or even in such deadly pandemics, as bodies were educated beneath a superstructure that defined associations with sulfur as preternaturally safe, as the senses of the Victorian Era and then twentieth-century sensory skills were cultivated to overcome any worry about evil getting in the way of profit (Otter 2008; Chari 2015).[5] As Brian Frehner has offered of sensory observations of American oilmen of the Second Industrial Revolution, "Knowledge about petroleum existed as theories in the minds of geologists as much as it took form in the physical labor and sensory experience of practical men" (2011, 47). As Section 4 offers for later eras as well, in the American West of the late nineteenth century, "Drillers and geologists generated different kinds of knowledge because their encounters in nature provided them with distinctive blends of intellectual and sensory experiences that reflected their unique epistemic goals" (2011, 75).

Investigating sulfuric toxicity through the senses then focuses a sixth section that consequently asks: How did modern peoples come to willfully accept ecological degradation? Capital works to destroy the detection of sensory

---

[5] For coal in North American development, see Bezís-Selfa (1997); Adams (2010); Pluymers (2016).

threats, hiding pollution in the opaque earth, counting deaths without attribution to the structural mess created by the wealthy, while also using discourse to numb the detection of sensory threats caused by fossil fuel production. As well, public activism and citizen-sensing movements, unifying data collection actions involving citizen activism in the absence of governmental support, are also inhibited due to the ability of capital to position their ecological violence upon populations that rarely have the power to resist the slow violence of toxic accumulation (Nixon 2011). Movements must become respected by the media and the public, through data as in the case of Aotearoa's resistance to corporate overreaches, in order to be deemed able to speak against fossil fuel companies, which are always initially deemed more in-the-know concerning the needs of society and threats of scarcity (Bond, Thomas, and Diprose 2023).

Despite possible resistances from somatic work and citizen-sensing movements that use data to challenge fossil fuel narratives, sulfur emanates evermore, the violence of climate change increases upon the earth, and the means of production continue to make bodies believe that sulfuric toxicity is natural and necessary, while at the same time mining and scarring the earth with increased automation that further destroys natural worlds and their human bodies (Parenti 2012, 43–56; Stengers 2015, 79–86; Wallace-Wells 2019, 109–118). As Gernot Wagner and Martin Weitzman offer in their analysis of environmental change, including increases in sulfuric atmospheres, humans must find new ways to come to terms with the unflinching global "climate shock" that has, to this point, become unmanageable to the global system and discourses required to manage its abusive forces (2015, 92–123).

2 Sensing the Devil in the Early Modern Era

With its threatening blue flames and rotting egg smell, often from hydrogen sulfide, the element of sulfur has, for centuries, been linked with beliefs about the underworld and concepts of the afterlife. The sensory attributes of sulfur have also been connected with volcanic activity for much of human history. The Greeks believed that Hephaestus, the god of fire and volcanoes, lived underneath Mount Etna in Sicily. As well, the Romans alleged that Vulcan, their god of fire, existed underneath Vesuvius (Meyer 1977; Turner 1993; Kroonenberg and Brown 2012; Kutney 2013).[6] Many associations between volcanic activity and mythical life also exist in diverse global cultures, and sulfur dioxide detection is often considered vital for multiple understandings of the "signal" of "a volcanoes mood" prior to a possible eruption. Sulfur content in ice cores also relay to vulcanologists much about the past of global atmospheres and the

---

[6] For more on hellish odors see Camporesi (1991, 76–80); Seiler (1992, 132–140).

Figure 3 This watercolor from Manuel María Paz (1820–1902) provides an image of Laguna Verde in southwestern Columbia. The green, here of a natural providence, comes from iron and sulfur sediments deposited in the volcanic region. Many modern industrial processes that use sulfur also often turn nearby waters or run off tailings into different greenish colors from the toxic compounds that escape from commercial mining enterprises. Colombia, Comisión Corográfica Sponsor, and Manuel María Paz. View of the Green Lake, Túquerres Province. Colombia Nariño, 1853.Courtesy of the Library of Congress.

links between sulfuric airs, disease outbreaks, and cultural readings of darkness and cultural themes about entering portals to other realms (Oppenheimer 2023, 10, 99–107) (Figure 3).

From approximately 1500 to 1650, English references to sulfur's stench focused on these prominent and intercultural sensory indications of hell, demons, and wickedness in worldly environments (Brant 2004; Harte 2023, 7–38). Throughout the Early Modern Era, the idea that sensing sulfur signifying evil or malevolence faded. Before that significant shift, prosecutions for sacrilegious behaviors, commonly read within English legal and religious circles during the early seventeenth century, often included attributing perceptions of brimstone to deeds of demonic worship (Preedy 2022, 115–122; Kettler 2024).[7] In the movement away from universalizing spiritual terminology of the Church to the disseminated literatures of the Reformation theatre, early modern politics, and the social world of intensifying capitalism, patterns of semantic dispersion and semiotic slippage provided many new desacralized meanings to previously numinous environmental perceptions (Brentjes and Schafer 2020).

Analyses of sulfuric meanings in the Early Modern Era are surprisingly substantial, often involving questions of Catholic malefactors attempting to kill James I with the Gunpowder Plot of 1605, latent folk traditions of witch-craft, and ideas of fumigation and skin treatments that applied sulfuric salves (Harris 2009; Friedman 2016, 100–118; LeCain 2017, 23–66). On the Shakespearean stage, squibs made of sulfuric content were often used to excite audiences to questions of faith and morality, while also tempting their rational-ity as a viewing audience (Preedy 2022, 156–172). As E.S. Mallin also points out concerning *Macbeth* (1606) in these frames of squibs and explosions, "perception is always, in this play, and in early modern theory, factored by rationality and morality." For Mallin, the play submits not only a history of witches, and their sulfuric presence related to the Gunpowder Plot, but also a tale of derangement whereby the perceptual apparatuses are so damaged within the play as to have Macbeth kill his own guards and allow for the individual insanity of sensing witches as real in the world (2016).

Thinking across much longer time periods concerning alterations in con-sciousness allows for a greater grasp on the valorization of capital that has altered bodies to experience the world in only specific, and bourgeoisie appro-priate, manners. This reading is vital in rethinking disenchantment as a historical thesis (Lander 2016; Josephson-Storm 2017; Joas 2021). Estrangement from the material world became common in the Early Modern Era due to abstractions caused by the subtle intensity of the new and forceful economic system as it informed personal relationships and altered cultural learning (Swarbrick 2023, 233–244). Modern bodies often desire a re-activation of the link between humans and elemental life to overcome the disassociations caused by capitalism and its brutal relations with the earth. As Jeffrey Jerome Cohen and Lowell Duckert offer, "The elements extend an invitation to stumbling, stuttering, to getting stuck in the past or not getting things precisely right. The temporality they convey is an enfolded one, poly-chronic, an invitation to play with knots" (2015, 17). Turning more to internal and uncanny aspects of sensation allows for a clearer reading of how

---

[7] See also the analysis of sulfuric violence upon the senses within Holmberg (2013), the reading of historical memory related to industry within Murray (2017), and hygienic projects using sulfur in Engelmann and Lynteris (2020).

disenchantment occurred over a *longue durée*. Such work can overcome much poststructuralist work on disenchantment that has become trapped in specific times and spaces, unable to value changes to embodied understandings (Boehrer 2015, 166–172; Martin 2015, 56–77; Kettler 2024).

The moral topography of medieval and early modern European spaces involved considerable integration of religious narratives into embodied experiences with ecology. This propensity is represented in all three sections of the *Garden of Earthly Delights* (1510), specifically involving the dark smoke of the pit of hell on the panel representing the moral topographies of the underworld. Narratives of miasmic evil entering the Garden of Eden, as in the other panels of Hieronymus Bosch's famous work, were common throughout medieval art and literature, portraying a cleanly heaven and a hell full of thick airs that also integrated into personal beliefs about profuse atmospheres and cleanliness in the lived world (Bintley and Franklin 2023, 110–120). In late medieval Europe, smell generally functioned through a binary system based upon cultural education concerning good and evil and foul and fragrant. Odors were also vital for diagnosis and treatment of diseases and were specifically related to scholastic thinking that often moved beyond religious identities. In most of these fields of understanding, the devil was believed to be detected through sulfur and other bad smells, often as the heat of bad odors and sulfur was linked to an internal heat that the lustful on earth could not control (Cockayne 2007; Robinson 2019, 157–182).

For older examples that led to such thinking within the literatures of the sixteenth century, in the Life of Martin, from Martin of Tours of the fourth century, a trickster figure adorned in jewels tempted Martin, and upon leaving the room, left the cell "with a great stink, a certain sign left behind that he had been the devil." In the work of the Venerable Bede, relaying Dryhthelm's visions from Melrose Abbey in the eight century, "vaporous flames" were central to the descriptions of hell, a tormented world that included "an incomparable stench that boiled out with vapors that filled all those shadowy places." Vision literature of many monks in the Middle Ages commonly offered such smells from demons that Dryhthelm particularly offered: "surrounded me and tormented me with their burning eyes and breathing putrid fire from their mouths and nostrils" (Robinson 2019, 162–163).

Religious descriptions portraying sulfur and brimstone as emitting hellish miasmas dominated atmospheric discourse before the Reformation (Classen 1992; Evans 2002; Foyster 2010; Newhauser 2016). It was widely believed that the oracles of Delphi, as within earlier writings from Cicero and Strabo, breathed in miasmic airs that came from deep in the underworld before exhibiting their divine inspirations (Ossa Richardson 2013, 19). In the frequently read

Renaissance text *Picatrix*, from the Arab author Ghāyat al-Ḥakīm and composed in the eleventh century, demons were also believed to possess bodies after burnings that created smoke from "hawk brains, mouse brains, and cat brains, mixed with sulfur, myrrh, and crane feces" (Koenig 2019, 220). Demonic sin also smelled of sulfur to medieval and early modern Europeans, whether from original sin or the supposed heresies of Jews or wayward Christians. The presence of bad air was also believed to create evil atmospheres that were unconducive to Christian learning and the discernment of good and evil, as exposed in the works of Pierre Bersuire. As Katelynn Robinson shows in recent work on smell in the Middle Ages, in *The Cloud of Unknowing*, a mystical text from the fourteenth century, the devil was believed to be a trickster who has only one nostril, signifying their undiscerning nature, where humans have two nostrils to discern good and bad smells and the good and bad behaviors signified by those aromas and odors. It was widely believed that if someone were to investigate the single nostril of the devil, they would see sulfuric fires and be driven instantly mad (Robinson 2019, 163–164, 194–195, 202–203).

Like monks facing hell in vision literature throughout the medieval world, as also within the works of the Monk of Evesham from the late twelfth century, encountering pungent brimstone in later European settings continually signaled some otherworldly evil presence. The *Malleus Maleficarum* (1487) specifically summarized the possible apparitions of devils that could be created by demonic spirits in the lived world. Flowing on dense vapors from beneath the earth, demons birthed from hell were deemed to emit sulfuric vapors and diverse atmospheres of brimstone (Preedy 2022, 90–92). For many engrossed through beliefs in the supernatural, these sulfuric sensations, often linked from histories of the sulfuric emissions God sent to destroy Sodom, were also commonly perceived on peoples existing in the liminal state between earth and the supernatural. As such, witchcraft often involved the ideas that the body of the witch was stained by the smell of Satan due to residues of an unnatural congress (Bacon 1683, 68–70; Pynsent 1993; Dugan 2011).

These frequently gendered terminologies related to smell and miasma of witches flooded the texts of legal prosecution as well. The frequently interrogative Reginald Scot, summarizing and questioning earlier witchcraft texts by Leonard Varius, provided in *Discoverie of Witchcraft* (1584) that women "are so troubled with evill humors … that out go their venomous exhalations, ingendered through their ill favored diet, and increased by means of their pernicious excrements that they expel." To Varius, witches specifically, through these gendered odors, also "belch up a certain breath, wherewith they bewitch whomsoever they list" (Levin 2023, 52). Brimstone as a signifying miasma was commonly found in other witchcraft manuals, as also within the writings of Jean Bodin, in Richard Bernard's *A Guide to*

Grand-Jury Men (1627), and within *The Lawes against Witches and Conivveration* (1645). Although absurd to modern sensibilities, the truth of smelling and sensing brimstone was vital in the configurations of guilt and innocence not only for witches but also in cases involving the scold's bridle that many women considered to be gossips were forced to wear as punishment for their supposedly brimstony temperaments (Bernard 1627, 173, 221, 235; Authority 1645, 5–6; Bodin 1995, 155–156; Darr 2011, 231–232; Kettler 2024).

As R.B. Pynsent has offered in readings of smell and witchcraft for Eastern Europeans of the early seventeenth century, "The stench of anything infernal was no doubt conceived in contrast to the odour of sanctity." On the spectrum of scents in the early modern world, the odor of sanctity secured that the presence of God was near while any foul odor was generally considered to be ranging in the direction of moral evil (Pynsent 1993). Even as it was common for demons and witches to shape shift to avoid detection, they could rarely shift their internal souls that were linked to demons and the signifying scents of sulfur. Most Eastern European contexts of witchcraft in these settings involved links to sexuality, either through sinning through relations with a demon or through committing the act of adultery in general. As Pynsent points out in the beliefs of Eastern Europeans of the sixteenth century, "The stench of adultery may be identified with the stench of the devil, because lust is the chief sin, adulterous lust the chiefest, and in sinning our soul commits adultery with the devil. Not only our body, but also our soul acquires an ichtic stench" (1993, 626).

In Western Europe these perceptions were common as well, as connivance with the Devil, often involving dancing in flames that did not burn, could lead to blockages caught in the throat (or invisible strangulation) and a "terrible smelling breath" linked to hellish odors, as discovered within the prosecution of Maria Suretegui in Logroño, Spain of 1610 (Homza 2024, 26–28). Often, bad odors were associated with such collusions through the prominent use of toads within witches' concoctions. Such toads were often used for poisons but also were pressed to release specific liquids that were used for olfactory anointing prior to working with demons (Rojas 2025, 121–144).

As Hjalmar Fors has offered in a reading of the disenchantment of science and the decline of magical causality in European allegations of witchcraft, ghosts, and trolls,

> Witchcraft accusations and the weight they were given as juridical evidence serve as a powerful reminder that people of the late seventeenth-century defined reality quite differently from most who live in the early twenty-first century. The early modern body was subject to many influences. Not only could it fall ill and become the victim of sudden physical violence. It could also be bewitched and shape-shifted, even squeezed into a keyhole. (Fors 2015, 17–42)

There was such prominence in the belief of the shape-shifting ability of demons that some early moderns initially believed that gunpowder, with its sulfuric content, was part of a demonic inspiration, often attributed to a wayward German monk by the name of Bartold Schwarz. As any revelation, or invention of such important variety, "must be either from above, or from beneath," many theologians questioned the depths of power that could arrive from spirits, good or bad, that "certainly know more mysteries in nature than we do" (Hales 1673, 286–288) (Figure 4).

Witches were believed to smell of sulfur in numerous cases involving a range of evil acts, whether through a haunting that included a signifying rat that

Figure 4 Witches were commonly understood to control the power of the skies and be searched out through detecting sulfur and brimstone within demonic atmospheres. Here, from *De lamiis et phitonicis mulieribus, Teutonice Vnholden vel Hexen*, are shape-shifting witches, flying on a pitchfork, causing a thunderstorm. Artist unknown. From "De Lamiis et Pythonicis Mulieribus," 1489. Rare Book and Special Collections Division. Molitor, Ulrich, Active, Johann Otmar, and Lessing J. Rosenwald Collection. *De lamiis et phitonicis mulieribus, Teutonice Vnholden vel Hexen.*
[Reutlingen, Johann Otmar, not before 10 Jan, 1489] Courtesy of the Library of Congress.

smelled of brimstone after falling from between a woman's legs, the consistently articulated smell of sulfur that filled a room after a demon left, or even when supposedly infecting a beer manufacturing operation (H.F. 1645, 20–22; I.H. 1645, 3–4; Glanvill et al. 1681, 93, 149, 157, 164, 166; Gaskill 2005, 63–64). Sulfur's pungency and other associated odors signified mischievous supernatural beings for Englishpersons of the sixteenth century, and well into the seventeenth century for those who retained beliefs from popular customs. As well, early modern narcotics often involved recipes including sulfur, which reserved cultural links between abnormal behaviors and ideas about demonic inspiration, witchcraft, and the unleashing of "animal spirits" within even supposedly civilized persons taken by sensations from sulfuric materials (Salmon 1683, 146).

Despite some of these continuing connotations of sulfuric evil, the seventeenth century included more chimneys that increasingly burned coal from English mines. With the need to heat homes, produce beer, improve the firing of bullets with sulfuric gunpowder and smelt iron, the supernatural associations of sulfuric sensations wavered. Literature responded to the demands of markets by acquiescing to a changing regime of the senses, as many authors began to mock sulfuric evil, unknowingly contributing to a greater acceptance of toxic compounds at the base of the Industrial Revolution. Before that significant change in the core, massive alterations in consciousness began to strike colonialist minds of the periphery, where the witches that were once at home and haunting in the metropole were seen more in the souls and bodies of those global savages perceived to need colonization and the new markings of cleanly Christianity (Taussig 1992; Cervantes 1994; Stoler 1995).

3 Sulfur, Othering, and Early Modern Empires

The displacement of Indigenous ways of knowing the environment partially occurred due to demonic attributions that worked to subordinate Indigenous knowledge when compared to the supposedly objective science of the emerging West. Sulfur was vital in these manipulations, as the attributes of brimstone were used to mark global others as indolent and consequently not able to inherit the right to judge how to respect or use the environment when compared with Western Europeans. The colonialist regime of perception shifted sulfuric evil to the periphery of the emerging world system in the Early Modern Era, whereby any sensing of sulfur in the colonial world generally meant that Indigenous spaces, always produced in diverse forms of consciousness rather than solely experienced by the colonizer, needed Christian conversion and the new gods of European capitalism to improve the profligate landscape, a common discursive practice of colonialism prominent within understandings of manipulative influences concerning sensation within diverse colonialist trajectories (Bashford 2004; Childers 2005; Shotwell 2011).

Through forms of sensory imperialism tied to language, Europeans worked through uncanny and purposeful manners to place upon the colonial world a signifier of demonic inferiority that had to be rooted out from the portentous earth. Disenchantment continued as a process of colonization through these atmospheric shifts, whereby the core started to secularize through making the periphery magical enough to need to be conquered by more rationalizing Western minds. As Nandini Das and Nick Davis have portrayed for the seventeenth century, such processes of disenchantment, whether in the core or periphery, often included vast changes within literary fields of power that provided changes to atmospheric contexts (2016).

Because specific sensations, as with smell, function in ephemeral atmospheres, their connotations can shift quickly and impact the body with great power born of cultural learning (Serres 2009; Ogawa 2021; Perras and Wicky 2021). Those quick changes impacted vast populations of the New World quickly after the arrival of Columbus and his sulfuric arquebuses in 1492. For colonized populations facing new categorizations of sulfuric influence in the centuries to follow, smelling their worlds had often included different connotations than what Westerners began to impose upon the New World through gunpowder and silver mines bleeding out brimstone airs. As Barbara Mundy has shown for the Nahuatl, the encounter included an Indigenous worldview in Central America that included a perception that smells penetrate and alter the body, even as Europeans of the Early Modern Era worked to deny allowing those penetrations under the belief that an open body was one threatened by demons, humoral imbalance, and disease (2021).

These colonized populations quickly learned that Westerners would bring atmospheric violence and new labor regimes through both material controls and alterations in how to understand perceiving the world as it changed beneath their feet (Lane 2005; Betancour 2017; Gomez 2020; Bigelow 2020; Studnicki-Gizbert 2022). The study of atmospherics is vital for encapsulating the general belief that air and the language attributed to the atmosphere causes experiential alterations. Modern atmospherics focus often on the role of institutional power and the stimulus of architecture on bodies and their emotional and perceptual experiences (Hasse 2014; Griffero 2016; Böhme 2017; Rosa 2020). Atmospheres, whether in colonial settings or more general senses of modern institutional construction, are often involved in the creation of shared emotions of the collective of bodies existing in diverse spaces. Shared emotions in these spaces educated by the language and beliefs of those in the space can be positive, cathartic, and triumphant but can also lead to the madness of crowds, partly created through manipulations in atmospheric content, both emotional and material (Trigg 2021). Atmospheres envelope human bodies, in the modern sense panoptical, but historically also for the creation of categories of power related to the body's immersion in a space for the desires of specific populations (McCormack 2018, 17–34).

For studies of colonialism in the Early Modern Era, the body has often been central to understanding the perception of colonized environments and atmospheres as other to European sensory understandings (Kupperman 1984; Chaplin 1997). Often, these colonial atmospheres signified disease through medical understandings of miasma and infection that predated bacteriology (Harrison 1996; Johnston 2013; Seth 2018). Recent scholarship, often through readings of Frantz Fanon, has begun to link such colonial histories of the body, especially from the perspective of the oppressed, with atmospheric analysis of how the airs that are breathed are coded and partially materialized by colonialism (Anderson 1995; Chiang 2004; Rotter 2011; Sharpe 2016; Yusoff 2018; Clare 2020; Hsu 2020; Calvillo 2023).

Atmospheric analysis, through relations of colonialism, portrays diverse universalizing categories of power that battled within different cultural discourses at the outset of modernity. In the crucible of the Caribbean, in the New World for Europeans, atmospheres of the colonized were often considered to be inspired by demonic influences. Those influences were believed to be sensed by Europeans, who for centuries prior, as explored in Section 1, had been able to link their understanding of religious texts to the power of their perceptions to encounter and detect evil in the lived world (Taussig 1980). Europeans entering these colonial spaces came to also understand that inserting a new means of production would assist in the project of rooting out the devil, altering the New World into a battleground supposedly fought over by pious and civilized Christians and demonically inspired Native Americans (Taussig 1992; Redden 2013).

As Walter Mignolo extends in many essential works on the body and colonialism, "There is no modernity without coloniality." The discovery of the New World and deeper spaces of sub-Saharan Africa furthered an accelerating reorganization of the senses within Western consciousness, whereby ethnographic thinking was used as a pharmacological remedy to the shock of discovery, creating a new self and other and the perceptual alterations necessary to birth a new ethics of modernity through networking of trade and behavior in identifiable and categorizable manners (Mignolo 2011, 2). As Nadia Altschul provides through reading of Domingo Faustino Sarmiento's *Facundo: Civilization and Barbarism* (1845) as a text exposing European understanding of their past colonial endeavors, the Western sense of "temporal layering is upheld and derives from differentiating what belongs to the medieval past and what belongs to the modern future" (Altschul 2020, 94–118). To mitigate a sense of fearful astonishment at varied encounters within colonial contact zones during the Early Modern Era, Europeans performed an intentional manipulation of sensory beliefs and temporality that stated Indigenous knowledges of the environment were inferior to Europeans, and justified their beliefs by stating Indigenous bodies were ripe with the odors and sensations of sulfuric hell that placed their consciousness in previous perceptual worlds.

A significant aspect of natural philosophy of the Early Modern Era allocated the Native American and African as part of the past through associating many of those societies as part of different, static, and earlier sensory worlds. Often, these ideals were also linked with Orientalist tendencies about the Middle East and East Asia, whereby anywhere the early modern European went to explore or colonize they discovered no contemporaries, asserting other bodies were trapped in the past. Sensory excesses deemed of the past, and of this colonized variety, were associated to ancient worlds to portray European civilization and the use of increasingly ordered perceptual schemas headed by vision as more sophisticated systems on the ladder of cultural evolution (Campbell 1999, 23–67; Taylor 2004). The shock of discovery created a sense of confidence for those who traveled and for those who began to think of engineering places of the discovery into newly patterned models of attempted neo-Europes. Many narratives of the New World and Africa included such confidence in planning to overcome any supposedly inferior colonized epistemology and elaborated upon sensory excesses of the rhetorically homogenized other that became increasingly trapped in the past both discursively and materially due to colonialist powers of military, market, and medicine.

Vast examples of sensory excess found in European travel narratives highlight these sensory constructions as they became structural, categorized, and oppressive, whether they were consciously narrated for policies of imperialist dominion or initially a recuperative product of the deep wonder caused by the shock of discovery. Linked with categories of Orientalist ontology, these ideas of sensing exploded into the taxonomies that increasingly controlled New World areas increasingly filling with Africana slaves and policies that suppressed and dominated Native American labor through slavery and repartimiento and then within later strategies of serfdom on encomiendas and bondage on plantations (Hulme 1986; Schiebinger 1993; Morgan 2004; Gaudio 2008).

For many Europeans, especially the French and British, Native Americans supposedly applied a much different sense of smell than the purportedly refined European. Nearly animal in their skillfulness, Native Americans and other aboriginal populations were believed to be able to hunt and practice warfare through their noses alone and were often said to be under the control of demonic leadership due to this reliance on the nose in a dense and dark nature (Kettler 2016). These false sensory skills to the Western European were progressively deemed disproportionate to the proper and civilizing sensorium of visual replicability through experimentation and helped many Western writers to define the colonized world as a place where the lower senses functioned through pre-modern and irrational modalities, often signified by the cannibalism commonly read in European intellectual circles from the writings of Michael Montaigne and Jean de Lery that placed cannibalistic cultures into indolent, demonic, and prelapsarian spaces (Montaigne 1700 [1580], 322–325; Lery 1990 [1578], 82–89; Klarer 1999; Bumas 2000). Only the higher sense of vision with the figures and calculations of constructed science, in contrast to irrational smells and tastes of human bodies and strange New World animals, could bring about a modern sensorium within Europe and within the institutions controlling her colonies.

Europeans entering greater colonial planning in the Early Modern Era believed many spaces of the world included atmospheres that threatened the inhabitants, and traveling Europeans, with demonic miasmas. Persia and Italy, to Lambert Daneau, included atmospheres of pestilence and evil vapors due to the non-Protestant practices of the people who lived in those spaces (Daneau 1575, 32–35). The African coast, on the Atlantic Ocean, was understood to include dense sulfuric airs that wafted onto the sea and could influence and sicken sailors passing too close (Herbert 1634, 6–8; Bohun 1671, 203–204; Kananoja 2016). The Middle East, especially areas of modern Israel, was believed by English Bishop Thomas Watson to still smell of the sulfur God used to destroy ancient Sodom and Gomorrah (Watson 1671, 112–113). In Ceylon of the late seventeenth century, it was believed by many English travelers that cattle were avoiding grazing near a demonic tree, signified to observers through the smell of sulfuric evil (Weekly 1682, 86).

The worldly categories of the atmospheres of the devil found throughout spaces desired by colonialists for conquest and profit became most prominent in the New World, and Native Americans in those spaces of early Spanish, French, and English contacts, were often believed to be informed by hellish influences that included sulfuric airs (Wafer 1903, 46 and 100). Often, the skies of hurricanes, a term from Indigenous roots, often involved Europeans framing the influence of the devil in the threatening storms. The writings of Fernández de Oviedo in *Sumario de la natural historia de Las Indias* (1526) include many of these observations of early Spanish travelers in the region. In Oviedo's contention, the devil was believed to be "a former astrologer" who could alter the skies and airs when Spaniards and Native Americans were actively not following the Lord's commandments (Myers 2010, 174–175; Schwartz 2015, 14–24). As interpretations of hurricanes show from confused Europeans, and also found within the writings of Peter Martyr that relayed Indigenous weather prediction as demonic and Native Americans in Panama as confused by Spanish cannonade as akin to a lightning storm, sulfuric airs were consistently linked to Indigenous ceremonies, which justified for Europeans even greater searching out of supposed Indigenous evils throughout the Americas (Martyr 1912 [1516], 111–112, 274–276; Kettler 2022)[8] (Figure 5).

Conquest narratives commonly relayed similar justifications through notations on the presence of sulfur, whether concerning the wandering devil who influenced the Tepehuan Revolt of 1616–1620 or within summaries of Aztec religious practices involving the purposeful cultivation of a sulfuric "Air-spirit" to counter the Spanish intrusion (Alarcón 1984, 62–63, 112, and 330; Ribas and Reff 1999; Kettler 2022). Such torments of the devil would often become perceived as audible in early Spanish churches in South America, where many would hear barking like dogs, braying like bulls, and hissing like serpents from what were believed to be devils besieging the Church (Toelle 2017). Consistently repeated imagery of demons above worshiping and wanton Native Americans alleged an atmosphere of evil secured through offerings provided to the pitchfork wielding, horned, and obscurely headed beasts in command (Figure 6).

Through creating categories of sensation based on inferior evils and moral superiority, the Western modernization process asserted its own history as a valorized praxis, whereby types of ethnographic and religious history were used to define Western power to rule through a legitimacy narrative that increasingly linked supposedly inferior races and nations to specific past spaces of inferior sensations and evil airs in purportedly scientific texts. Race scientist Arthur de Gobineau, in multiple publications from 1853 to 1855, argued that the supposed body odor of non-white races was evidence of these supposed aspects of inferiority that trapped Indigenous populations of the world into a past of sensory indulgence instead of European refinement. The race scientist also asserted that Africans, as with other supposedly lesser races, were specifically better equipped to detect harsh tastes and smells and had much greater tolerance for evil smells that Europeans would generally deem to be overpowering. For Gobineau "smell" in the societies of Africa and other Indigenous regions was "developed to an extent unknown to the other two races." Such definitions came from texts of earlier centuries and led to later perceptions that Africa itself

---

[8] For more on hurricanes in the Atlantic World see Johnson (2011).

Figure 5 Native Americans in the expanding Spanish Empire of the seventeenth century were frequently portrayed as linked to the devil, and, as with the imagery here from cartographer and Jesuit priest Alonso de Ovalle, as being punished for their blasphemies by the atmospheres of the recently arriving Catholic God, sainted warriors, and angels from overhead. Indigenous populations, for this image concerning idolatry in Chile, were portrayed as living among demons through the relaying imaginaries of hell and devilish connotations, including snakes, tails, hydra, and the sulfur smoke from a nearby volcano. Alonso de Ovalle, *Historica relacion de reyno de Chile] Historica relacion del reyno de Chile, y delas missiones, y ministerios que exercita en el la Compañia de Iesus* (En Roma [Rome]: Por Francisco Cavallo, 1646), plate; following p. 302. Courtesy of the John Carter Brown Library.

smelled of diverse odors related to savagery, including the African ability to scent out threatening animals, smell-out witches and demons in the jungle heat, and produce often miasmic and sulfuric atmospheres that Europeans understood as totemic to define a heretic landscape (Gobineau 1915, 204–205).

Figure 6 This print portrays an example of a Native American ritual from the transnational French perspective, appearing in Johann Justinus Gebauer's 1752 translation of Joseph François Lafitau's *Mœurs des sauvages ameriquains, comparées aux mœurs des premiers temps* (1724). The imagery again depicts a floating and miasmic demon above Indigenous ritual practices, here supposedly portraying initiation rites whereby Native American awoken by the noise of the demonic appearance observe their diabolic supervisors and the atmosphere surrounding the devilish figure. Johann Friedrich Schröter, Siegmund Jakob Baumgarten, Joseph-François Lafitau, and Pierre-François-Xavier de Charlevoix, *Algemeine Geschichte der Länder und Völker von America.: Erster [-zweiter] Theil*, trans. Johann Justinus Gebauer (Halle: Bey Johann Justinus Gebauer, 1752), plate 15; vol. 1, following p. 160. Courtesy of the John Carter Brown Library.

The ravaging of colonial environments, today existing under the rubric of the Resource Curse, involved, at their outset, significant linkages between racialization and the prominence of the rhetorical civilizing mission in diverse regions. As Mohamed Amer Meziane points out, secularization in the cores was driven by the initial forcing of religion upon the periphery, whereby the making of modern geologic advantages for Westerners involved accumulations in colonized regions that were justified by the shifting of racialization and ideas about inferior religious beliefs upon the Global South. Europeans sacrificed the magical spaces of their core ideologies to tie their future to the worldly goods of empire, creating secularization at home while inventing the new gods of capital to abuse global populations abroad (2024, 1–12, 255–278). Western Europeans valorized their conquests through a self-referential historical worlding that stated supposed intellectual ingenuity allowed for the prominence of the nation-state to rise and conquer the colonial world. Rather, accidents of energy and nearness to specific materials led to the ascension, even as the false narrative of European innovation persists through valorization today (De Landa 2000, 71–102).

The great divergence that created the modern economy out of northwest Europe rose due to the nearness to coal, and associated sulfur, nitrogen, and timber supplies that became the basis of the modern maritime trading economy at the center of the world system. Europeans, with the land of colonial settings to ravage, did not need to organize internal lands through absolutist and forceful control on their own populations, creating a "freedom" in the Western world that did not exist in the East because the Western world used the lands of the Global South, and continues to use those lands, for resource management with much greater force than within the domestic setting (Pomeranz 2000, 3–28, 52–67). That rise of Western economics and epistemologies could not have occurred if Europeans had not moved into the colonialist settings where they justified their actions through shifting moral concerns from the core outward upon the colonized. Sulfuric connotations that crossed Catholic and Protestant lines and national backgrounds involved the frequent marking of Indigenous cultures as satanic, which also positioned the ways of knowing in those cultures, the ways of perceiving ecologies, as flawed. Throughout the Early Modern Era, whether in New Spain or in Salem, Massachusetts, where teenage girls smelling of sulfur were deemed evil, demons and witches left the Old World for the New World, as Europeans believed they were cleansing their homes through Reformation or Counter-Reformation, and consequently shifted the invisible worlds of their pasts upon bodies to be colonized in the name of progress throughout the world (Koslofsky 2021).

European perceptual apparatuses made the world into a tragedy for many populations in these five hundred years of Western colonialism, in part through marking subaltern ideas about the environment as inferior. That discourse continues today, as nearly all non-Western or non-positivist thinking about environmentalism and climate change is understood or framed as feminine and implausible by the means of production. Forms of planetary longing peer out from beneath such Western thinking about structures, patterns, and the need for more energy within systems that arose out of such environmental manipulations at the base of modern control societies. Other epistemologies rage from beneath and must be accorded weight in these chaotic moments of global warming that threaten life on earth with existential risk for individuals and collectives (Pratt 2022). The politics of being able to breathe in the warming world, and who has the right to breathe clean air, is a continuation of decolonial and anti-colonial resistance movements from centuries since the rise of modernity in the crucible of the Caribbean. The planetary forces of Indigenous resistance to imperialism and the importance of local sensory knowledge as a way to resist capital map a pathway to engage with guerilla forms of perception in support of the earth against the patterns of increasingly automated extraction, against pollution and sulfuric toxicity, and in favor of collective healthfulness (Dietrich 2017; DeLoughrey 2019; Lauer 2023).

As Patricia Widener offers in modern context of New Zealand and the need for a broad multiscalar lens for understanding the history of ecological colonialism and modern environmental decay, "Recognizing the importance of place infuses additional meanings into rural, coastal and aquatic environments and the living beings affiliated with those spaces, and reveals layers of privilege and oppression imposed on a people and place by industry proponents and opponents" (Widener 2021). Energy worship that denies the rights of Indigenous and local epistemologies is common in the modern world and emerged out of an Enlightenment obsessed within extreme rationality that positioned value above nearly all other interests. Networks of value, human and nonhuman, emerged out of the great coal profits of the nineteenth century to position a modern fossil fuel industry of significant individual reliance, including a dependence on the networked market that, in turn, created a new form of servitude in the name of energy that displaced non-Western ways of knowing (Debeir, Deléage, and Hémery 1990, 87–133; Nikiforuk 2012; Ghosh 2017, 62–82).

4 The Devil's Demise

Accelerations of modern climate change began with primitive accumulation in colonial spaces, as Europeans justified ecological degradation and human sins through the valorization of capitalism as a new system for the greater benefit of all persons. Wherever colonialism accelerated, climate disaster followed. In the wake of those disasters, whether on Caribbean islands that Columbus and his men depleted of food supplies, in the toxic waste of sulfur compounds and mercury caused by Spanish mining operations, or in the massive deforestation for many colonial projects throughout the New World, the colonialist system linked with valorizing capital to avoid having to concern itself with the damage.

Each new step forward in colonialism further justified greater and superior hiding of ecological sins and faster accumulations at the edge of the Anthropocene (Fressoz and Locher 2024, 11–26, 259–262).

Back in the core, secularization took hold. As the magic of the world moved to the periphery, the core found the new gods of capital and the end of supernaturalia in the environment appropriately linked for a stronger push into economic modernity, impacting material observations and beliefs about faithfulness. Sulfur, in these contexts, lost most of its supernatural associations. The European past of mystical connotations existed within a relatively singular belief system based in Catholicism. Reformation discourse opened a sense of questioning concerning that centralized focus on mysticism (Robertson 2009; Pickett 2011). Altering worldviews moved sulfuric associations from the frequently singular to the plural, and the multiplicity of sulfuric links shifted not only to include contemptuousness of the devil, which had existed prior in medieval literature, but also within a fuller breadth of metaphors and meanings that did not exist in the same way within those earlier iterations (Crawford 2017; Baum 2019; Kettler 2024).

The declining place of odor as a spiritual signifier generally allied with a Protestant shift that moved the devil from a space in worldly atmospheres to a character that was battled deep in the psyche (Clark 1997, 8–10 and 174–176). As the devil moved into the mind, and out of the environment, Protestant demonism accelerated into more ardent fire and brimstone articulations that retained some physical aspects of the devil but more so denied the existence of the devil in the lived spaces of the world. In general, without the prominence of environmental evidence to maintain guilt or innocence, even of fabricated varieties, proving or disproving the devil became much more a battle of wits between accusers and the accused that was based on power relationships (Johnstone 2004). Spurring, and existing alongside, these psychological alterations, many early modern plays began to mock the idea that sulfur meant the devil or the presence of evil in the environment. *Gammer Gurton's Needle* (1575), *The Puritan: Or the Widow of Watling-Street* (1607), and the *Witch of Edmonton* (1621) specifically included parodying tones to the idea that sulfur was inherently demonic when sensed in worldly environments. These secularizing and comedic tones of the public sphere and literary worlds led to a further displacing of perceptions of evil from natural surroundings (Stevenson 1575, 7–9; Pudney 2019, 45–57; Kettler 2024).

Although categories of medieval literature had included comedy that critiqued the Church, those criticisms became more potent and diverse with the rise of the Reformation and into the age of the Industrial Revolution (Manley 1995, 432–436). While *Gammer Gurton's Needle* maintains many religious inferences, the play applies irony about the devil during a moment of historical change, as the Reformation rerouted the tones of comedy to a mocking that existed within a society that included multiple choices of religious belief beyond accepting Catholic supernaturalism. Akin to other humors of stench, invention, and sanitation of the era, as within John Harrington's *The Metamorphosis of Ajax* (1596) or Ben Jonson's *The Alchemist* (1610), mockery about bodily functions, privies, and smell was often applied as part of a cultural "coping mechanism" that included a "disarming preemption" during eras of disenchantment from previous convictions about miasma within earlier English society (Bowers 2013, 56–60). Numerous texts in the public sphere paired with literature that mocked smells as signifying witchcraft or able to be used to battle against demons. William Perkins' *Discourse of the Damned Art of Witchcraft* (1610), John Cotta's *The Infallible True and Assured Witch* (1625), and John Weemes' *A Treatise of the Foure Degenerate Sonnes* (1636) all included denials that demons could be perceived in the lived world through the cultivation of human sensation, referencing the emanations of brimstone and sulfur as absurd to be relied upon when engaging with an opponent as wily as the devil (Kettler 2024).

Shakespeare's works were no different in their sulfuric complexity. In *Macbeth* (1606), especially with the opening chant of the play involving the letting off of smells for the audience that "penetrated the physical space of the theatre," a common catharsis would be cultivated to influence harrowing fears of the supernatural and the natural born through a public sphere on the edge of modern sensibilities (Theile 2016, 84; Liebler 1995). As Chloe Kathleen Preedy also offers of these playhouse manipulations, "as new playhouses brought the sky and local atmosphere into perceptible presence, the dramatic works staged within alluded to and interacted with the air in increasingly overt and evocative ways." In many areas, miasma was linked with diverse aspects of medical contagion, and sulfuric odors were believed to be part of a threatening atmosphere for those engaging with the theatre (2022, 10; Greenblatt 2002) (Figure 7).

The darkly comedic plot in James Shirley's *The Maides Revenge* (1626), involving a murderess accidently ingesting poison, provided the sinful with taste and convulsions from the toxin that portended, through their sensations, "the dark foggy way that spits fire and brimstone" into nethermost hell (Kuhn 2024, 159). Such inherent complexity of sulfur on the theatre stage of dark comedies helped lead to a rise in metaphor as divorced from the real world, a distancing that also led also to the emergence of even more joking folk-tales about the devil, as with the history, relayed by Thomas Newbigging in later eras, about Hell Gill, also known as the Devil's Bathtub, which is marked by a hill of stones that supposed fell out of the devil's apron pockets when he was forced to

Figure 7 Early modern plays, as with *Hamlet* and ghostliness portrayed here, often used stage direction and explosives squibs to signify the sensory changes of catharsis for the audience. Many squibs were made of sulfuric content that offered diverse associations to disenchanting audience members. For *Macbeth* and *Hamlet*, many of these atmospheric references coincided with beliefs about the natural, preternatural, and supernatural connotations of sulfur and brimstone. Robert Thew, Artist, and Henry Fuseli. "Shakespeare–Hamlet–Prince of Denmark," painted by H. Fuseli, R.A.; engraved by R. Thew, 1796. London: Published by J. & J. Boydell. Photograph. Courtesy of the Library of Congress.

rise from a bath and tore his clothes due to the need for speed. Numerous such early modern popular folktales of the devil dying after tripping down a mountain in Northumbria or drowning in the Tyne became quite popular in the eighteenth and nineteenth centuries, especially in the West of England. As Jeremy Harte offers "these stories put the Devil in a contemptible, often comic light: they are pantomime, slapstick." Rather than a threat in the environment, the devil was dead, and often died in mostly comic manners, killed by ecology as the English took their landscape from God and the devil and provided it to the new gods of industry and capital (Harte 2023, 58–59).

Such supposedly purgative patterns did not only arrive with the conglomerate corporations of the last century but existed at the core of capitalism during primitive accumulation of fossil fuels in earlier eras, whereby discourses about a person, place, or thing can be manipulated by the superstructure to allow persons, places, or things greater space to commit ecological or social violence upon the base. As wealth from the use of coal, and its sulfuric impurities, grew during the seventeenth and eighteenth centuries, social discourses altered to construct new laws able to subdue citizens wishing to damage coal supplies, mines, and forests. Whether citizens were producing beer from coal-fired ovens, gathering coal to sell to manufacturers, igniting the processes of coal firing to make iron at the head of the Industrial Revolution, or accessing coal for warmth in English towns, they seldom encountered sulfur as a determinant of demons (Evelyn 1661; Tryon 1682; Hiltner 2007; Cavert 2014).

Despite early ecological concerns with sulfuric airs and the clouds that floated above seventeenth-century cities, like with royal anti-smoke campaigns in London, most of the public sphere came to accept coal as necessary for better beer, faster production of iron, and greater wealth for the English nation and the later British Empire. As William Cavert has asserted, cheaper coal often burned in dirtier forms, which made specific sulfuric pollution a highly local concern rather than a national issue. Dirty, smoky, air was commonly understood as problematic in the capital in 1600, as high-sulfur and cheaper bituminous coal was commonly used by the poor for heating homes and for beer kilns (2017, 34–39). As the Whiggish progress of history continued, royal concerns of conspicuousness became proportionally less powerful. Western populations came to accept the pollution of sulfuric compounds through changes in the lived world that manifested within literature and social discourse. Even as many scientists increasingly came to understand the threats of sulfur, including within John Arbuthnot's *Essay Concerning the Effects of Air on Human Bodies* (1733) and through the writings of William Harvey in the later eighteenth century, commoners still came to consent to sulfuric pollution because capitalism needed that contaminant to be allowed for the better success of English nationalism (Cavert 2017, 80–93).

That general public in the West was also convinced by other scientists in a mostly uncanny defense of capital, as with Thomas Willis in the seventeenth century, who sometimes offered, with numerous physicians in his camp, that sulfuric airs in the atmosphere could clean the lungs. Enough of such thinking and the disenchantment of religious ideals related to sulfur led to a public sphere of the late eighteenth century that distrusted some scientists in favor of others, and displaced the idea that sulfur was threatening with enough force as to grant the market and the state inordinate power to pollute the skies. As Cavert notes, over the scientific revolution, "discoveries and innovations" related to coal smoke "made it less, rather than more, certain whether and how coal smoke constituted dangerously bad air." An abundance of theories allowed pollution to seep into daily life due to the lack of scientific consensus, a common rhetorical trick potent in modern greenwashed media. Exposing where in discourse such discursive slippage occurs is often occlusive, but still can be exposed with a focus upon subtle changes in superstructural messaging over significant moments of historical change (2017, 93–99; Engelmann and Lynteris 2020).

The market and military needed sulfur to be considered a positive as the product was necessary for coal-firing and filling the muskets of the New Model Army and its more advanced derivatives. As such, a grand discursive and uncanny manipulation began, whereby sulfuric signatures moved from being considered a pollutant that emitted the signs of hell to a fetish that signified cleanliness through fumigation and an important odor that meant Britain and other Western European powers were leading the march of progress within the capitalist global order (Cavert 2017, 35–37). The myriad uses for sulfuric materials, increasing with bituminous high-sulfur coal in the late eighteenth century, offered smells, taste, sounds, and burns of hell, but were increasingly considered only through connotations of progress even as sulfur dioxide of the nineteenth century often filled the skies to nearly seventy times the current amount within the airs above London (Brimblecombe and Grossi 2009). As Peter Thorsheim notes of the nineteenth century when such blacked-out skies in London became common, it was regularly believed that "the carbon and sulphur it contained were seen as fumigants that could neutralize miasma. Within this context, people looked at coal smoke not as pollution, but as something that could help to protect against it." Such that in the late 1840s, it was commonly believed that inhaling the sulfur of coal smoke was a cure for tuberculosis. Even as investigators came to understand sulfur as a pollutant that caused acid rain, within discussions of the later nineteenth century, those deliberations rarely moved into issues of demonic evil or significant concerns with human health, focusing instead on threats to buildings and urban beauty (2006, 16–18).

Such diachronic readings of sulfur specifically upset synchronic thinking concerning much recent literature on disenchantment, while emphasizing that histories of perception can demonstrate changes in physical understandings of the world as ideologies about influences upon the environment shifted over time. As faith about the supernatural instructions upon the lived world faded during the Reformation, certain textual signifiers remained from Catholic super-naturalia within the lexicon, but their power in the phenomenological spaces of daily life were increasingly weakened. Shadowy and murky English paths advanced into spaces made to hear gunpowder blasts, taste brimstony waters, and smell the miasma of sulfuric fumigation without perceiving the threats of the devil (Johnstone 2006; Kitch 2016) (Figure 8).

Figure 8 Sulfur is also included in many modern military applications, linking a longer tradition that included sulfur as one of the three main ingredients in original black gunpowder with the modern warfare of atmospheric violence from bombs and toxic smokes. "This weird figure is a chemical warfare man carrying two Sulphur Trioxide smoke bombs" (U.S. Air Force Number 23490AC). National Archives. Record Group 342: Records of U.S. Air Force Commands, Activities, and Organizations, 1900–2003. Black and White and Color Photographs of U.S. Air Force and Predecessor Agencies Activities, Facilities and Personnel-World War II and Korean War, ca. 1940-ca. 1980. Courtesy of the Library of Congress.

5 Brimstone Frontiers

Geology faced a historical evolution since the Renaissance, becoming a rapid and critical form of the New Science that informed how Europeans understood the world beneath their feet. Bringing questions of the self and other into European perceptions of geologic materials that were to be mined highlights the lack of agency that was provided to both the material earth and subaltern bodies in those contexts. During the early seventeenth century English beer manufacturers and iron smelters began to rely on sea coal to increase their economies of scale to meet growing English populations (Hiltner 2007). By the nineteenth century, geology and capital linked even further to create a new and dominant worldview of sulfuric material, as with the digging up of coal and other soon to be fossil fuels that did not include significant questions of sensing the devil (Kettler 2020).

In early modern contexts, the devil's metal of sulfur was also related to quicksilver, and alchemists believed for centuries that the rock was essential in the production and cleaning of nearly all metals. This was so well acknowledged by early modern Englishpersons that *The Garden of the Muses* (1610) stated in poetic verse that every metal was "of Sulphur made" as an analogy to certainty (Bodenham and Munday 1610, 27). The medieval alchemist found much use for sulfur as essential in their hopes of discovering the higher wisdom they believed they could learn from the writings of the original biblical prophets, in part with the desire to turn other metals into gold. Usually living as both monks and scholars, many alchemists understood the mercurial and unstable nature of sulfuric compounds. Alchemists, using the works of Paracelsus, generally defined sulfur as one of three basic primes to produce chemical reactions in other metals (Croll, Pinnell, and Paracelsus 1657, 120–123; Goodrick-Clarke 2008, 75–78).

Significant for the change in geologic contexts for Western Europeans were colonial experiments that offered new information about geologic worlds that upset earlier biblical ideas. As the historian Joaquin Perez Malero proposed for the Spanish Empire in the New World, a general scientific shift occurred from a natural philosophy of geology based on classical theory and biblical readings to a more applied geology tied to mining and profit. For Malero, this significant shift took place between 1640 and 1761, between the work of Alvaro Alonso Barba in *Arte de los Metals* and Fransisco Xavier de Gamboa in *Commentarios a las Ordenzanzas de Minas*. Between 1450 and 1550, considerable changes had already initially moved from earlier alchemical learning about metals to a more focused and applied mining based upon silver production and improvements in hydraulic power, as found within Georgius Agricola's *De Re Metallica* (1556). Spanish mining lagged behind technologies of mining in the mineral rich areas of Germany, Austria, and northern Italy where Agricola, born Georg Bauer, had studied. As such, when miners in the Spanish Empire began their projects in the New World, they were generally behind concerning innovations, and consequently had to work more laborers in often inefficient manners. The search for gold initially, and then much more for silver into the sixteenth century, prompted the Spanish to rethink mining culture away from cosmological concerns toward much more profitability and the accelerations of displacement regarding Indigenous concepts of metallic cosmology or subaltern ideas about sensing ecologies (Melero 2009).

The growing value of sulfur for the general welfare and for industrial and military applications did not fit the singularly sacred metaphors used to define a sulfuric devil disembarking his sycophantic allies that was proportionally prominent during the sixteenth century. The scientific revolution had linked with the need for profit and progress to alter sensory worlding within broader epistemologies (Salter 2010; Chico 2019). Into the seventeenth and eighteenth centuries, mining manuals and geologists found much greater truth in marking specific sensations within scientific searches for coal using the detection of sulfur (Plattes 1679; Strachey 1727). Tied to these profitable searches, investigations of sulfur in the environment became increasingly common during the seventeenth century and developed as central to scientific study during the eighteenth century, whereby sulfur, frequently used in scientific work, increasingly emerged into prominence due to greater secularization. Isaac Newton specifically was obsessed with sulfur and sulfuric compounds, thinking often about what products created internal fires of the earth, planets, and stars, impurities in iron, and more complex arrangement of bonding that made sulfur the base of all metals within alchemical traditions, and informed later issues of metallic generation deep in the crust (Newman 2019, 27–29, 188–189, 198–207, 243–245, 287–288, 314–349, 382–414, 443–464, 480–488, 506–514).

Such advancements led to greater state controls, in Western Europe especially, over technical understanding of compounds, especially related to sulfuric combinations of explosives and energetic mixtures of fossil fuels (Thébaud-Sorger 2018). Knowledge of sulfur advanced in later chemical experimentation during the eighteenth century, much in the West through the work of French chemist Antoine Lavoisier. Lavoisier, before his execution by guillotine, discovered that sulfur, like other elements, cannot be created or destroyed in chemical reactions, but can only be transformed from one form to another. He also determined the nature of sulfuric compounds, and demonstrated that sulfur, when burned in air, combines with oxygen to form sulfur dioxide gas, which he then studied in detail, laying significant foundations for modern chemistry (Lavoisier 2011 [1790]).

Due in part to connotational shifts in fields of defense, science, and medicine tied to advances in chemistry, coal mining burgeoned, driving the brick kilns of beer manufacturing into beehive ovens, puddling techniques, and the grander furnaces of pig iron smelting advanced by Henry Cort, Dud Dudley, and Abraham Darby (Freese 2016; Kander, Malanima, and Warde 2017). These technological advances continued into the eighteenth century through the coke-burning blast ovens for the steel mills of the Industrial Revolution and the eighteenth-century coal-fired weapon designs of John Wilkinson. By the middle of the nineteenth century, and within earlier secularizing works, most English references to sulfur consequently associated the rock to medicine, warfare, and pharmacology, leading to debate on the scientific nature of sulfur within geologic texts that no longer included references to hellish sensations (Henckel 1757, 134–162; Colbatch and Tuthill 1689, 55–69 and 83–88).

Susan Neiman has specifically articulated the focus on "evil" within debates of the later Enlightenment around the Lisbon earthquake of 1755, as many began to question the nature of malevolence that arose from "natural" disasters, as from the earth, and those from more causal and human forces (Neiman 2015, 1–13). Seismology and geology kicked any of the "evil" associations of its work to become a considerable aspect of disaster science in the centuries to follow, as within a general society increasingly devoid of associations to the hellishness of sulfuric airs released often in earthquakes and volcanoes (Coen 2013). Through a capitalized process of valorization of new mining and energy regimes, disenchantment of the role of spiritualism in the environment took even greater hold over Europeans, whether Protestant or Catholic, through a process that accelerated out of the Early Modern Era into a nineteenth century when literature tied in even greater links directly to narrative development in support of capital and mining interests (Miller 2021, 24–36). As Richard Read also shows, this new profitability of geology and middle-class interests in geologic science led to alterations in the sense of sight related to landscape painting and modern aesthetics (Read 2022). In this unstable and cruel modernity of the emerging capitalists, as Veronica della Dora has also asserted, "the surface of the earth reflected back not only patterns of light, but also different ways of seeing and thinking about the environment." For many, the earth shaped human geography, forcing populations to develop in specific spaces with explicit cultures. For other observers, what became prominent in modernity was the acceleration of human controls on such geological and geographic influences of where people could prosper (della Dora 2021, 1–14, 163–232, 232).

Coal and iron were pivotal to the base of the Industrial Revolution, and the sulfuric by-products burgeoning near those advancements combined to build a Western ability for greater and quicker travel, both by ocean and overland. Capitalists used metals like iron, from burning sulfuric coal, to build better mail coach networks, bridges for highways, construction for carriages, and heated inns at distant highway stops. As Jack Goody offered concerning the influence of coal and associated metals on social development, extraction and smelting created the physical power of modern capitalism while generally also driving an Enlightenment focused on engineering and construction of an imperialist military power of the streamlined productions of gunpowder and the cast iron needed for weapons manufacturing (2012, 249–284; Kelly 2009; Brugh 2019).

On the North American frontier, increasingly devoid of supernatural significations, sensory skills were consequently applied not to sense the devil or his minions, but to engage a new and profound search for minerals. As frontiersmen pushed west, invading Native American territories while they defined their selves against the landscape, they taught each other how to root out sulfur and coal as both a threat to water supplies and as a positive for profit (Valencius 2004, 109–132; Carter 2018, 29–64; Kettler 2020). Those travelers that set out for western American reaches avoided such connotations for evil, as the natural was increasingly devoid of any evil, and outlined the importance of mineral reserves to the expansion of the British Empire, American nationalism, and the Canadian frontier. Threats and opportunities were vital on these early frontiers and as far to the west into British Columbia, and the education of the senses taught settlers where to look and what to avoid. Their notes consistently contained the importance of coal, with persistent attention paid to the skills learned to analyze the sulfuric impurities of the product commonly understood today in diverse industrial literatures (Wynn 2007; Watson 2016) (Figure 9).

In Britain and the United States, those who could harness the coal and steam that voyagers would use on the high seas were heroes of the Industrial Age (Smith 2018, 172–178, 204–224, 304–322). Often these valorizations also took Anglo and American merchants to southern reaches to engage in profiteering on Latin American and southern African mines of the nineteenth century (Maxwell 1902; Monteon 2019). As Stephen Mosley has noted of industrializing eras of the nineteenth century that coincided with these reaches and the ships that came to global ports of an emerging world system powered by coal and steam, "unlike the foul odours associated with miasmas," coal smoke "did not fill the Victorian city dweller with apprehension. Indeed, many people actively embraced the idea that this form of air pollution deodorized and disinfected the urban atmosphere" (2001, 84). That deconstructive shift, in part in the core, partly shifted to the colonies, and then manifested through the destinies of supposed progress in the American west, allowed for sulfur's smells to permeate life in more profound ways, leading to crisis concerning ecological threats from sulfur that include coal smoke in the lungs, acid rain from the skies, and cancerous sulfuric compounds finding their way into drinking water (Ashby 1981; Brimblecombe 1987; Montrie 2003; Casner 2005).

Despite early movements to point out the sins of capitalism upon world ecologies, the engine of capitalism pushed forward, powering over early environmentalism of the late nineteenth century and placing more burdens on the backs of workers in Western cores and abused peripheries. Laborers the world

Figure 9 Western travelers in North America frequently used sulfuric
sensations to detect either impure water or the profits of coal seams that were
often signified by hearing, tasting, smelling, or seeing sulfuric compounds.
"Along Big Sulphur Creek in the Maycamas Mountains of Sonoma Country,
near Geyserville and Cloverdale, California, March 23, 1852," pencil, sepia and
wash on beige paper. John Russell Bartlett, 1852.
Courtesy of the John Carter Brown Library.

over faced manifestations of sulfuric disease as fossil fuels became the mark of
modernity for nations within the new world system (Robins 2011; McIvor and
Johnston 2016). Early nineteenth-century coal labor in the United States was
often completed by American slaves, and into more modern ages of supposedly
free labor coal and sulfur mining is still completed in extremely threatening
conditions both in the Global North and in the Global South. In one instance of
a coal fire underneath Black Heath Pits in Virginia of 1810, attempts by slave
laborers to douse the flames were met with, as one observer noted, "incredibly
strong" airs of "Sulphur" that led those who "had not been down five minutes …
to stagger & fall from the effects" (Lewis 1979). Slaves faced the misery of such
dizzying work, explosions that led to blinding, death in the mines from mercury
poisoning, and lasting impacts traced to the leeching of sulfuric matter into
nearby ground water throughout American history at the edge of Civil War

(Silkenat 2022, 20–32). As Lara Cohen has offered, semiotics of the underground in the United States began to include much more than rocks, mining, and demons due to these links with the violations of the peculiar institution. The underground, tied to the underground railroad as a subversive metaphor, became increasingly associated as a space for resistance for slaves during the 1840s and 1850s. Mammoth Cave, in Kentucky, specifically became a literary site for the interplay between ideas of the enslaved "subculture" and the need for an "underground" to hide from masters. The site later converted into a cultural point of reckoning for runaways and many enslaved guides who led white populations through the location (Cohen 2022, 1–45, 74–103).

The world system based in fossil fuels articulated the goal of abundance at great peril to ecologies and laborers, as sulfuric coal was carried on the backs of slaves, proletariat, and precariat bodies facing diseases from increased atmospheric noxiousness. Whether from silicosis, tuberculosis, or black lung, work in mines where sulfur compounds also caused toxicity became common in a twentieth century marked by a Western world that reaped the benefits of capitalism. These advantages for the West often arose through impositions of nominal democracy within the antidemocratic Middle East, even as the laborers of the Global South become linked evermore to a planetary mine with burdened subalterns facing pollution as a mark of colonialism, whether national or corporate interests racing for the last of fossil fuel resources on earth before absolute worldly exhaustion (Klare 2012, 209–234; Mitchell 2013; Gomez 2020, 191–222) (Figure 10).

The burgeoning nineteenth- and twentieth-century goal of extracting phosphates for the creation of fertilizers, applying sulfur for food and wine preservatives, or for using sulfur to produce bactericides further drove Western states to cordon off large portions of the world's sulfur supply through vast mercantile, corporate, and mining manipulations. This penchant for sulfur markets driven by narratives of capital valorization was exemplified by the Sulfur War of 1840 fought throughout latently mercantilist economies and including military preparations throughout Europe. Centering near the volcanic regions of the Mediterranean coast, sulfur mines often employed children, *carusi* in Sicilian, who bore the burden of sulfur's weight on their hunched backs when moving the rock from covered shafts to aboveground stores (Ferrara, 2015; Cunha, 2019; Kettler 2024).

Sulfur progressed scientifically with explicit chemical applications for the rising capital needs of the modern world. Invented by Charles Goodyear in 1844, sulfur vulcanization involves mixing sulfur with rubber before forming into shapes, as with tires. Vulcanizing rubber creates stronger, more durable products (Slack 2002). Most of these industrial uses for sulfur, including

Figure 10 J.M.W. Turners' *Keelmen Heaving in Coals by Moonlight* (1835) portrays the coal and sulfuric life of nineteenth-century England using mysterious light. The painting portrays keelman of Tyne and Wear, those laborers who had to move coal from the side of the harbor to waiting kilns in larger collier ships off the Northeastern coast of England. These draught keels and their men were a prominent aspect of English life in the nineteenth century. Turner's work portrays heat and light to provide atmospherics of the existence of such workers who, even with a moon high in the center of the painting, work in the dark of coal and sulfur smoke to the right. J.M.W. Turner, *Keelmen Heaving in Coals by Moonlight* (1835). National Gallery of Art. Public Domain.

vulcanization, were aided in the late nineteenth century due to the invention of the Frasch process in 1867, which uses superheated water to extract sulfur from underground deposits, increasing the numbers of miners and laborers that faced sulfuric smells, sulfuric toxins, and sulfuric sensations (Haynes 1959).

As Elizabeth Carolyn Miller noted of the realist novels of the English countryside, as with George Eliot's *Mill on the Floss* (1860), literature specifically altered to accommodate greater and quicker extraction through these processes and innovations, often through supporting narratives of mining in different global spaces of a new imperialism. Capitalized literatures offered increased coal consumption, and coal and sulfur as cleanly within narratives, as a necessary tool to overcome the exhaustion of laborers unable to keep up with industrialization without steam power assistants, commonly articulated in works like John Holland's *The History and Description of Fossil Fuel* (1841) and W. Stanley Jevons' *The Coal Question: An Inquiry Concerning the Progress of the Nation, and the Probable Exhaustion of Our Coal-Mines* (1865) (Miller 2021, 24–36; MacDuffie 2014).

Industrialization of coal and fossil fuels in the United States also led to an intensification of sulfuric airs on both laboring bodies and communities near factories and mines, due partly to such scientific and narrative justifications. As Shepherd McKinley notes of Charleston, South Carolina, a prominent region for phosphate and sulfur use, "drawbacks included residential complaints and lawsuits about smells and noxious fumes associated with fertilizer manufacturing." Into the twentieth century, an era that also saw the growing use of sulfur baths, vacations to sulfur spas, and sulfur soaps on grocery shelves, runoff from large factories near Charleston led to ocean leaching of phosphates and airs of sulfuric compounds that impacted environments while at the same time creating modern Southern agriculture and the booms of cotton towns after the end of American enslavement (McKinley 2014, 131 and 153–166).

As Megan Black has shown, the search for sulfuric minerals and compounds at such areas, and throughout the American Sun Belt linked to increased governmental funding, gradually involved direct links between private power and the rise of the military industrial complex through the Department of the Interior in the United States. That department, alongside the American army, moved their interests from domestic to global issues of mining throughout the twentieth century, using endeavors and experiments in diverse regions to expand private companies the ability to mine in nations that faced the intensification of the Resource Curse (Black 2018). Such "wastelanding" of mineral regions of the world, first domestic and then global within diverse networks of both illegal and legal waste trading including toxic waste and consumer waste, primed the United States, with Western capitalism of the world system, to expand into the lone superpower at the end of the Cold War (Voyles 2015; Clapp 2024).

The American superpower made profit the basis of accelerating to frontier markets using energy found from within the earth. Part of that expansion involved vast attention to the smelting of copper, which produces considerable amounts of sulfur dioxide. Britain had produced half the world's copper by 1856, which grew to a considerable market due to the need for copper wires to transmit telegraph messages. Later copper production led to atmospheric and wastewater contamination as sites for smelting grew throughout the world, increasingly in Chile and Cuba throughout the twentieth century. The

American copper industry had grown in the middle of the nineteenth century as well, centering around Cleveland, Tennessee, mostly due to the nearness of large coal supplies for fuel from Appalachia. Each roast of coal and firewood that was used to smelt copper in the open air during that era "produced a million pounds of sulfur gas" (Stoll 2022, 77–81, 91–93).

The role of copper and sulfur has recently become of even greater importance due to the shift toward renewable and battery energy within modern economies. Early batteries from the 1890s often involved the bathing of zinc, copper, or mercury in zinc sulfate or copper sulfate in battery cells lined with paints made from rubber and naphtha. These large batteries had to be refilled twice a week, and the used substances were often dumped in nearby waterways before the rise of any environmental protection sentiments. Lithium, copper, cobalt, rare earths, and nickel are mined in increasing weights for use in diverse batteries of the modern world and for development of future technology and rising forms of Artificial Intelligence, furthering sulfuric toxicity as necessary for the economic base (Stoll 2022, 77–81).

This "new oil" of products used to power batteries has led to a race to promote lithium mining throughout the Americas, which include the large Thacker Pass Project and the planned Rhyolite Ridge operation by Ioneer in Nevada. Lithium mining and production involves the importation of hundreds of thousands of metric tons of sulfur on a yearly basis at each large mine once developed, as sulfur is used to leech lithium from the sedimentary rock in the region, also creating vast amounts of stinking sulfuric steam (Scheyder 2024, 131–134, 187–190). Numerous corporations attempting to enter these battery markets try to create "zero discharge" from their sites nominally, but, as with Freeport copper mines near the Arizona and New Mexico border, sulfuric toxins often still leak, leading to lawsuits from those having to live in the polluted areas (Scheyder 2024, 211–217).

Such advances, despite their values for technology and economic growth in the Global North, have left many modern people, especially laborers facing the abusive resonances of sulfur deep within the remnant mines of Java, choking from lungs incrusted upon by once evil sulfur floated into the coal hazes of modernity. Java and its burdened workers have been for a century at the basis of modern geologic science and plate tectonics, as the "pulse of the earth" attracted many Western scientists to the region, which has only burdened more workers who have been situated to labor in volcanic spaces considered to produce some of the finest sulfur on the planet (Bobbette 2023).

Literature about the environment can change ecological perceptions (Williams 1975; Cohen 2015; Farrier 2019). During the Early Modern Era bodies increasingly accepted toxic atmospheres into the Industrial Revolution, partly through changes in language that made the evil and toxic into the acceptable. Laborers faced silicosis and other lung ailments with little acknowledgment of their cause. Within literatures that linked science, manufacturing, and narrative entertainment for the masses, sulfur proportionally shifted from associations with the evils of the Devil to more potent links with the grandeur of nationalism, positivism, and the march of modernity, marked in texts and perceived in the senses of each unwilling player on a procession marching into an Anthropocene currently burdened with a lack of clean breathing (Engelmann 2020; Albano 2023).

6 Sulfur Shifted, Sulfur Contained

Similar patterns that create the fetish, whether through valorization of capital or constructions of commodities as proper to be consumed, occur through a libidinal and networked economy of sensory associations to luxury and comfort that alter embodied experience. In this manipulation caused by networks of language and meaning, the superstructure also alters sensory associations of the body to not sense that which might threaten economic relationships (Appadurai 1988; Lyotard 2015; Massumi 2015). Within these discursive processes that create sensory agnotology, the manufacturing of ignorance or unthinking acceptance in social organization, humans are consistently concealed away from understanding the declining spaces of nature, partly through discourse that alters the function of sensation to remove or discard specific relationships that would tend toward greater embodied understandings of threats to the earth (Douglas 1966; Marshall 2014, 226–238; Morton 2019, 60–62; Lepawsky and Liboiron 2022).

When you smell sulfur, think capital, divorced from links to the devil because it was profitable to the bourgeoisie. Disenchantment of sulfuric materials from those hellish links took centuries. Now, capital sends sulfuric compounds the world over, into water tables, into the air, and the world misses those devilish occurrences because capital has also altered our bodies to not be able to perceive the threat as anything akin to the previous evils of a supposed Satan. The masses are modeled, have the senses educated, by networks of capitalist existence to mature into sensory passivity. We deny, with our very bodies, that we are participating in a system that destroys the earth. Sulfuric airs poison our bodies, sulfuric compounds infect the earth, and sulfuric molecules degrade our water. Yet, we accelerate onward with cheap gas in our tanks.

We produce these sulfuric compounds in chemical combinations from a scientific culture that has come to accept the profitable habits of energy in the age of petroculture and petrostates, and we salute and valorize the political operatives that kneel before corporate leaders of American, Middle Eastern, and Western European fossil fuel conglomerates. We deny the suffering caused by fossil fuels because it is habituated in our sensations to welcome the compliance of our sensory worlds. We find a sulfuric sensory worlding in modernity because sulfur was re-organized linguistically over the Early Modern Era, taking brimstone from a previous position outside the bounds of accepted consumption and into a novel space within the discourses of the Industrial Revolution.

Readings of disenchantment often suggest that scientific modernity that arose with a separation of nature and society should not be implicitly judged as positive, as with the basis of disenchantment that came from Weber, but, rather, that processes of capitalist enchantment instigated a modernity facing constant crisis. Such a process is understood herein, whereby disenchantment occurred, but not in the sense of a rising and wondrous positive creation of the Rankean civilizing processes. Rather, secularization simply harkened in a new era of enchantment, a shift from the importance of the Christian God in the environment to a space of modernity where the gods of capital influence nearly all worldly encounters with ecological materials (Thomas 1971; Latour 1991; Bennett 2001; Walsham 2008; Waldron 2013; Floyd-Wilson 2013).

We need to re-educate our sensory skills to again understand sulfuric emanations as sensory threat, even as capital works to degrade those sensory apparatuses so humanity does not sense the concerning airs of modern life and the agency within geologic objects (Rosner and Markowitz 2002; Bennett 2010; Bogost 2012; Morton 2014; LeCain 2017; Chen 2014). This does not need to be understood as a religious threat, a demonic presence, but the inability to see the evil in fossil fuel acceleration the world over rises from earlier desensitization caused by secularization and desacralization processes of modern capital. With the myths of capitalist valor accelerating, coal pollution causes cancer, autism, miscarriages, and poor lung and brain development in children, and infects miners throughout the world with sulfuric toxicity that invades water tables and local agricultures (Curran 1993; Derickson 2014). Often, these toxic spaces of modern life in the world system link with Environmental Racism, as bodies racialized into specific spaces often find a lack of governmental awareness and even more distance from the levers of power to be able to transform against ecological decline (Spears 2014).

In Japan, a nation beset by a toxic past linked to nuclear weapons and an intensive speed used for initial industrialization processes, sulfur compounds are commonly found to cause considerable disease environments. As Brett Walker summarizes concerning the Japanese attempt to clean such prominence of sulfuric compounds,

> sulfur dioxide, in even modest doses, is dangerous enough, damaging the
> respiratory system and causing bronchitis; but sulfur dioxide and its neutraliz-
> ing products ammonium bisulfate and ammonium sulfate usually take the form
> of metallic particulates, which in water droplets or on ash represent the most
> potent of atmospheric acids. Daily exposure to any more than 100 parts
> per million (ppm) causes chronic bronchitis in most people. (Walker 2011, 95)

With the traditions of industrial power, energy companies the world over impose disaster capitalism upon the body, whereby the sensorium becomes a demolished area of non-knowledge, commodified by capital that can profit with greater ease within the wastelands (Klein 2007).

The poetics of the Anthropocene are invaded by the powers of capital through terms like "clean coal" or through the limited material work done through flue gas desulfurization and carbon capture (Mudahar 1986; Douwe 2010; Glass 2016). Fossil fuel expansion continues to change the climate, heating the atmosphere to record levels, warming the oceans, killing bodies, spreading environmental alterations leading to stinking sulfuric sargassum, and melting the ice caps. Often, the advancement of the most toxic of capitalist enterprises continues unabated due to the offshoring of some of the more toxic industries from cores to modern capitalist peripheries in wastelanded areas of the globe where laborers cannot organize to resist the toxicity. Because of these manipulated discourses on health, geoengineering, ideas about environmental flexibility and the adaptations of ever valorized energy, often meant to create amnesia or exhaustion among those wanting to protect the environment, energy conglomerates continue hiding the sensory signatures of pollutants like sulfur, rather than removing most of those contaminants (Lockwood 2014; Wainwright and Mann 2018; Buck 2019; Thomson 2019) (Figure 11).

Historical regulations have been attempted, more in the West than in the colonized spaces of the world where Western colonialists could avoid much domestic concern through committing labor abuses on racialized bodies. State science arose in the early twentieth century of progressivism in the North Atlantic, partly driven from the regulatory mechanisms of the British state in the nineteenth century with the Alkali Act of 1863 that controlled amounts of sulfur compounds released in specific areas. Western states worked to later "geo-code" the atmosphere, such that in Britain of the 1950s government-sponsored reports helped to create the highly influential Clean Air Act of 1956 in response to the Great London Smog of 1952 and led to the impetus for the following Clean Air Act of 1963 in the United States (Whitehead 2011, 67–93, 126–155, 180–209).

In the United States, that later Clean Air Act helped to create a 1970s where environmentalists were able to impose significant controls on sulfuric airs, as

Figure 11 Modern industrial processes often involve sulfuric by-products, as sulfuric compounds are found in fossil fuels and are left after many industrial processes related to mining, as fertilizer production, steel pickling, rubber vulcanization, and chemical processing of sulfuric acid at copper mines that often exist on nearly barren ground due to toxic dispersion of sulfuric compounds. "Copper mining and sulfuric acid plant, Copperhill, Tennessee." Marion Post Wolcott, photographer. United States Tennessee Copperhill Polk County, September, 1939. Photograph.
Courtesy of the Library of Congress.

the recovery of sulfur dioxide became mandatory under federal law, partially due to the debates on acid rain common at the time (Rothschild 2019; Turner 2022, 42–44). Still, industry resists regulation, even with knowledge of the death and disease that industry causes, because of valorization narratives that articulate the naturalness of capitalism, even as the system imposes sulfuric airs upon choking lungs (Gardiner 2019). Modern regulators attempt to impart guidelines even after waves of neoliberal deregulation that followed such environmentalism throughout the 1980s, as with the Kyoto Protocols starting in 2005, recent attempts at the Paris Accords of 2015, at COP 26 in 2023, or through the earlier 2008 EU standards that attempt to curb emissions, but these programs often find implementation and enforcement upon capital to be increasingly incredible, often due to Western equivocations over the energy policies of China, India, and developing carbon economies (Kramer 2020; Guenther 2024, 110–145; Beynon and Hudson 2024, 7–30).

Even as some of the working class mourn the loss of previous industrial successes in specific global regions for familial and nostalgic reasons, as with the Black Country of England and the Appalachian coal regions of the United States, the most common forms of support or energy regimes come directly from corporate manipulations and bribes paid to leading policymakers, as due to the war on the environment and the constructions of flexibility and Cornucopianism within environmental discourse that began through mass lobbying during the 1970s (Felli 2021; Asprey 2021). This increasing impossibility to regulate arises partly due to a lack of public support, partially due to the belief in the lower prices that deregulation can provide. This "discounting" of environmental threat is a political technology linked to capitalist desires to dominate the present through manifesting a forgetting of the future (Doganova 2024). Public engagement is consequently key to thinking about sensing the ecological degradation caused by capital, even as populations the world over are blinded as a way to access cheaper gas that continues to drive the engine of capitalism. Much of public reluctance to do much about sulfuric toxicity, even when it is sensed, is also due to rhetorical and cultural links between specific impoverished populations and legacies of mining in specific regions, as in the aforementioned British midlands, or in regions facing frac sand mining in Wisconsin and hilltop removal in Appalachia (Pearson 2017; Francis and Groes 2021; Beynon 2024, 147–149, 344–352).

Regulation has failed in the past few decades as conservative forces have found ways around public concern and government reporting to create a neoliberal scheme of deregulation that allows for most ecological sins to go unnoticed or unprosecuted. In this modern world, uneven distribution of healthy breathing creates greater risk upon different populations. Due to contamination, weaponization, and monetization of air by the powers and profits of extractive capitalism, different population groups face pollution from sulfuric toxicity in uneven manners. A modern "crisis of breathing" has risen since the 1970s and is consistently portrayed in diverse artworks trying to expose the threats faced by racialized populations in the wake of such intensive deregulation (Tremblay 2022, 1–32).

Citizen-sensing movements, and the sharing of knowledge about the world and its decline through the senses, works against these goals of capital to hide its abuses in the obtuse earth and within manipulative discourse. Recent work to create networks of engaged citizens using drones and sensors to show the world the impacts of chemical and fossil fuel companies on lived atmospheres have become a central strategy in making capitalism pay for what it is doing to lungs and bodies. These modern forms of guerilla breathing involve more collectivist campaigns that reach greater exposure. As Jennifer Gabrys offers, becoming "sensing citizens" involves attending to technics "as extended relations and fields of influence" that make it "possible to create more constructive technological engagements that attend to pluralistic citizens, relations, milieus, sociality, and worlds in the making" (2022, 245–252; Berardi 2018, 130–145). As Gabrys proposes elsewhere in the context of sulfuric air and citizen sensing through data collection of particulates in the atmosphere, making data into its own creature with narrative force can provide new pathways for linking human sensory skills and sensing abilities to a formative praxis that gives information power as objects with social capital or purchase in the public sphere (Gabrys 2016, 157–169).

An embodied ethic of breathing in the world can allow for a more direct connection with polluting materials that capital wants to hide from human sensations. Performative aesthetics are already exploring breathing as a rebellious act in a world torn asunder by fossil fuel profits. Respiration is a human right that is being damaged by profitable energy regimes that exist outside of the democratic ethos, driving fascist and libertarian forms of capital without governmental checks that are powered by the people. Breathing in the air, and perceiving the toxicity within that air, allows for emotion and sensory affect to emerge from the embodied person. The current environmental moment must engage these ideals of narrative biophilia through understanding attention to sensory skills, whereby attending the earth, even though attention to the nonliving and toxic, will allow a more encompassed view of the damage being provided by unsympathetic polluters (Orr 2004; Wark 2015; Haraway 2016; von Mossner 2017, 137–163; Usher 2019; DeLoughrey 2019, 132–164; Taylor 2020, 245–250).

The law has often proven less than significant in regulating corporate interests in their use of toxic sulfur, necessitating new patterns on how to educate the public through the haze of misinformation and legal manipulation, as portrayed by the manipulative language used in the cases of gold mining in Colombia and the infamous track of the *Khian Sea* loaded with incinerator ash from the United States of 1986 (Müller 2023; Jonkman 2024). For the Ducktown Mining District in the Southern Appalachian Mountains of the United States, the ability to use formal governmental measures and lawsuits took nearly a century before significant alterations to regulations limited the consistent release of sulfur dioxide unconstrained into the air from the application of sulfuric acid for copper mining, even with victories for possible regulators in significant Supreme Court decisions originally in 1907 (Maysilles 2011). To persist within an Anthropocene that is increasingly polluted, hot, and plastic, society must remind the law and the body what sulfur is, an evil contamination to the body politic, rather than deny the exacting sensations of sulfuric compounds upon the body. As Deborah Hawhee has pointed out, "awareness and information have proven to be necessary but still insufficient for action" which necessitate "novel climate rhetorics" to imagine new futures (2023, 138–146; Lawrence and Laybourn-Langton 2022) (Figure 12).

How those futures are imagined must understand the sensory discourse of greenwashing that capital has used to commit its assault on the body. Renewable energy is one path to overcome that which capital has imposed but also must be

Figure 12 Copper mining involves intensive use of sulfuric acid. Here is a wasteland that has created a desert landscape in rural Tennessee. Common near copper plants due to the leeching of sulfuric acid, desert landscapes often exist where there had once been lush vegetation. It is widely noted in economic history that in the nineteenth and twentieth centuries industrial analysts often judged the success of a nation's economy on its amount of sulfuric acid used in manufacturing, as the product is essential in the making of numerous industrial goods. Marion Post Wolcott, photographer. Copper mining section between Ducktown and Copperhill, Tennessee. Fumes from smelting copper for sulfuric acid have destroyed all vegetation and eroded the land. United States Ducktown Copperhill Tennessee, 1939. Sept. Photograph. Courtesy of the Library of Congress.

wary of too utopian of impulses that the means of production also uses as manipulative force (Hughes 2021). The Anthropocene, and the more modern version of the automated planetary mine that scars the earth and accelerates the death of the earth, was allowed for, was accepted, was created through discursive shifts that started with primitive accumulation during the Early Modern Era. Sulfur marks those changes as the toxicity of numerous sulfuric compounds now invades everyday bodies. Would they if they were still considered evil? Would they if they could again be considered demonic? The planet becomes a mine without reconsidering what humanity senses as toxic, as matter out of place. The earth is evermore scraped by automated robotics that destroys labor markets and the ability of labor to negotiate, as in the Atacama mines of Chile so succinctly described in the networks of modern life by Martín Arboleda (2020, 243–260).

This planetary mine of automated machines the size of skyscrapers must be countered through human senses, the rights of the body, the ability to sense the toxic and warn the world of the evils of the capitalist and their desire dig deeper and automate (Morrison 2015). Westerners must also look to long overlooked aesthetic practices from Indigenous populations throughout the world to better assess how to cultivate sensory skills to push against these ravages of capital. Even as narrative power provides much greater force to political leaders' relations with fossil fuels, it is workers who must remain at the center of the energy narrative to best understand social developments of energy regimes and resistance to ecological decline (Santiago 2006, 205–255). In Central America and South America numerous ways of knowing the world have risen to resist capitalist extraction in Global South mining and agriculture zones. These cultural ways of sensing offer ways of living beyond the boundaries of capitalism that involve creating aesthetics that critique the energy edifices of the world system through ideas of escaping or moving beyond capital through diverse moral economies (Gómez-Barris 2017; Conty 2023).

The modern atmosphere has involved sulfur in numerous modern contexts, mostly arising from fossil fuels, but also involving the use of sulfuric odors placed upon odorless gases through mercaptans to allow for detection of immediate threats in the household (Williams 2021, 83–130). Climate change skeptics are altered in these moments to a siege mentality, often born of religious ideations that allow for the acceptance of unproven faith, which disallows their ability to change their own minds, choosing conspiracies instead of listening to common sense, sensing the world, or accessing reliable data (Haltinner and Sarathchandra 2023, 51–68). The "breathing catastrophe" of modern life which follows has led to even more attention upon atmospheres in the wake of Covid-19, as the threats of different and diseased and asthmatic airs are now commonly understood the world over. However, capital has maneuvered deftly in these times as well, pinning the sins leading to the ravages of Covid-19 upon the state, shifting blame for poor air, diseased air, and policies about the air away from sinning capital. Rather than blame the moneyed, many populations in the West have also shifted to conspiratorial thinking about why the air is becoming so damaging, unable to pin the tail on the palpable, broadest, stinking, and sulfuric ass of the quite obvious sinners among the bourgeoisie (Bonneuil and Fressoz 2016; Di Cesare 2021, 94–109).

References

Adams, Sean (2010) *Old Dominion, Industrial Commonwealth*: *Coal, Politics, and Economy in Antebellum America*. Baltimore, MD: Johns Hopkins.

Alaimo, Stacy (2016) *Exposed*: *Environmental Politics and Pleasures in Posthuman Times*. Minneapolis, MN: University of Minnesota.

Alarcón, Hernando Ruiz de (1984) *Treatise on the Heathen Superstitions that Today Live among the Indians Native to this New Spain, 1629*, ed. James Richard Andrews. London: University of Oklahoma.

Albano, Caterina (2023) *Out of Breath*: *Vulnerability of Air in Contemporary Art*. Minneapolis, MN: University of Minnesota.

Altschul, Nadia (2020) *Politics of Temporalization*: *Medievalism and Orientalism in Nineteenth-Century South America*. Philadelphia, PA: University of Pennsylvania.

Anderson, Warwick (1995) Excremental Colonialism: Public Health and the Poetics of Pollution. *Critical Inquiry* 21(3), 640–669.

Anderton, Douglas, and Susan Hautaniemi Leonard (2004) Grammars of Death: An Analysis of Nineteenth-Century Literal Causes of Death from the Age of Miasmas to Germ Theory. *Social Science History* 28(1), 111–143.

Appadurai, Arjun (1988) *The Social Life of Things*: *Commodities in Cultural Perspective*. Cambridge, MA: Harvard.

Arboleda, Martin (2020) *Planetary Mine*: *Territories of Extraction under Late Capitalism*. London: Verso.

Ashby, Eric, and Mary Anderson (1981) *The Politics of Clean Air*. Oxford: Oxford.

Asprey, Esther (2021) "Pack up Your Blarting": The Language of the Senses in Black Country Dialect. In R. M. Francis and Sebastian Groes, eds., *Smell, Memory, and Literature in the Black Country*, pp. 86-107. Cham: Palgrave.

Authority (1645) *The Lawes against Witches, and Conivration*. London: R.W.

Bacon, Roger, Duarte Madeira Arrais, and Richard Browne (1683) *The Cure of Old Age and Preservation of Youth*. London: Felscher.

Bashford, Alison (2004) *Imperial Hygiene*: *A Critical History of Colonialism, Nationalism and Public Health*. Basingstoke: Palgrave Macmillan.

Baum, Jacob (2019) *Reformation of the Senses*: *The Paradox of Religious Belief and Practice in Germany*. Urbana, IL: University of Illinois.

Bennett, Jane (2001) *The Enchantment of Modern Life*: *Attachments, Crossings, and Ethics*. Princeton, NJ: Princeton.

Bennett, Jane (2010) *Vibrant Matter*: *A Political Ecology of Things*. Durham, NC: Duke.

Bentancor, Orlando (2017) *The Matter of Empire*: *Metaphysics and Mining in Colonial Peru*. Pittsburgh, PA: University of Pittsburgh.

Berardi, Franco (2018) *Breathing*: *Chaos and Poetry*. South Pasadena, CA: Semiotext(e).

Bernard, Richard (1627) *A Guide to Grand-Jury Men*. London: Kingston.

Beynon, Huw, and Ray Hudson (2024) *The Shadow of the Mine*: *Coal and the End of Industrial Britain*. London: Verso.

Bezís-Selfa, John (1997) Slavery and the Disciplining of Free Labor in the Colonial Mid-Atlantic Iron Industry. *Pennsylvania History*: *A Journal of Mid-Atlantic Studies* 64, 270–286.

Bigelow, Allison (2020) *Mining Language*: *Racial Thinking, Indigenous Knowledge, and Colonial Metallurgy in the Early Modern Iberian World*. Chapel Hill, NC: University of North Carolina.

Bintley, Michael, and Kate Franklin (2023) *Landscapes and Environments of the Middle Ages*. London: Taylor & Francis.

Black, Megan (2018) *The Global Interior*: *Mineral Frontiers and American Power*. Cambridge, MA: Harvard.

Bobbette, Adam (2023) *The Pulse of the Earth*: *Political Geology in Java*. Durham, NC: Duke.

Bodenham, John, and Anthony Munday (1610) *The Garden of the Muses*. London: Edward Allde for John Tap.

Bodin, Jean, Randy Scott, and Jonathan Pearl (1995) [1580] *On the Demon-Mania of Witches*. Toronto: University of Toronto.

Boehrer, Bruce Thomas (2015) *Environmental Degradation in Jacobean Drama*. Cambridge: Cambridge.

Bogost, Ian (2012) *Alien Phenomenology, or, What It's Like to Be a Thing*. Minneapolis, MN: University of Minnesota.

Böhme, Gernot (2016) *The Aesthetics of Atmospheres*. London: Taylor & Francis.

Böhme, Gernot (2017) *Atmospheric Architectures*: *The Aesthetics of Felt Spaces*. London: Bloomsbury Academic.

Bohun, Ralph (1671) *A Discourse Concerning the Origine and Properties of Wind with an Historicall Account of Hurricanes and Other Tempestuous Winds*. Oxford: W. Hall for Tho. Bowman.

Bond, Sophie, Amanda Thomas, and Gradon Diprose (2023) *Stopping Oil*: *Climate Justice and Hope*. London: Pluto.

Bonneuil, Christophe, and Jean-Baptiste Fressoz (2016) *The Shock of the Anthropocene*: *The Earth, History and Us*. London: Verso.

Bostrom, Nick (2014) *Superintelligence*: *Paths, Dangers, Strategies*. Oxford: Oxford.

Bowers, Rick (2013) *Radical Comedy in Early Modern England: Contexts, Cultures, Performances*. Burlington, VT: Ashgate.

Boyer, Dominic (2023) *No More Fossils*. Minneapolis, MN: University of Minnesota.

Brant, Clare (2004) Fume and Perfume: Some Eighteenth-Century Uses of Smell. *Journal of British Studies* 43(4), 444–463.

Brentjes, Sonja, and Dagmar Schafer (2020) Visualizations of the Heavens before 1700 as a Concern of the History of Science, Medicine and Technology. *NTM: Journal of the History of Science, Technology and Medicine* 28(3), 295–304.

Brimblecombe, Peter (1987) *The Big Smoke: A History of Air Pollution in London Since Medieval Times*. London: Methuen.

Brimblecombe, Peter, and Carlota M. Grossi (2009) Millennium-Long Damage to Building Materials in London. *Science of the Total Environment* 407(4), 1354–1361.

Brugh, Patrick (2019) *Gunpowder, Masculinity, and Warfare in German Texts, 1400–1700*. Rochester, NY: University of Rochester.

Buck, Holly Jean (2019) *After Geoengineering: Climate Tragedy, Repair, and Restoration*. London: Verso.

Bumas, E. Shaskan (2000) The Cannibal Butcher Shop: Protestant Uses of Las Casas's *Brevisima Relacion* and the Case of the Apostle Eliot, *Early American Literature* 35, 107-136.

Calvillo, Nerea (2023) *Aeropolis: Queering Air in Toxicpolluted Worlds*. New York: Columbia.

Campbell, Mary (1999) *Wonder & Science: Imagining Worlds in Early Modern Europe*. Ithaca, NY: Cornell.

Camporesi, Piero (1991) *The Fear of Hell: Images of Damnation and Salvation in Early Modern Europe*. University Park, PA: Pennsylvania State.

Camporesi, Piero (1994) *The Anatomy of the Senses: Natural Symbols in Medieval and Early Modern Italy*. Cambridge: Cambridge.

Canales, Jimena (2022) *Bedeviled: A Shadow History of Demons in Science*. Princeton, NJ: Princeton.

Carter, Sarah Anne (2018) *Object Lessons: How Nineteenth-Century Americans Learned to Make Sense of the Material World*. New York: Oxford.

Casner, Nicholas (2005) Acid Mine Drainage and Pittsburgh's Water Quality. In Joel Tarr, ed., *Devastation and Renewal: An Environmental History of Pittsburgh and Its Region*, pp. 89–109. Pittsburgh, PA: Pittsburgh.

Castillo, Bernal Diaz del (1963) *The Conquest of New Spain*, trans. J. M. Cohen. New York: Penguin.

Cavert, William (2014) The Environmental Policy of Charles I: Coal Smoke and the English Monarchy, 1624–40. *Journal of British Studies* 53(2), 310–333.

Cavert, William (2017) *The Smoke of London*: *Energy and Environment in the Early Modern City*. Cambridge: Cambridge.

Cervantes, Fernando (1994) *The Devil in the New World*: *The Impact of Diabolism in New Spain*. New Haven, CT: Yale.

Chakrabarty, Dipesh (2023) *One Planet, Many Worlds*: *The Climate Parallax*. Waltham, MA: Brandeis.

Chaplin, Joyce (1997) Natural Philosophy and an Early Racial Idiom in North America: Comparing English and Indian Bodies. *William and Mary Quarterly* 54, 229–252.

Chari, Anita Sridhar (2015) *A Political Economy of the Senses*: *Neoliberalism, Reification, Critique*. New York: Columbia.

Chen, Mel (2014) *Animacies*: *Biopolitics, Racial Mattering, and Queer Affect*. Durham, NC: Duke.

Chiang, Chang Y. (2004) Monterey-by-the-Smell: Odors and Social Conflict on the California Coastline. *Pacific Historical Review* 73(2), 183–214.

Chico, Tita (2019) *The Experimental Imagination*: *Literary Knowledge and Science in the British Enlightenment*. Stanford, CA: Stanford.

Childers, Joseph (2005) Foreign Matter: Imperial Filth. In William Cohen and Ryan Johnson, eds., *Filth*: *Dirt, Disgust, and Modern Life*, pp. 201–224. Minneapolis, MN: University of Minnesota.

Clapp, Alexander (2024) *Waste Wars*: *The Wild Afterlife of Your Trash*. New York: Little Brown.

Clare, Stephanie (2020) *Earthly Encounters*: *Sensation, Feminist Theory, and the Anthropocene*. New York: SUNY.

Clark, Stuart (1997) *Thinking with Demons*: *The Idea of Witchcraft in Early Modern Europe*. Oxford: Oxford.

Clary-Lemon, Jennifer (2019) *Planting the Anthropocene*: *Rhetorics of Natureculture*. Logan, UT: Utah State.

Classen, Constance (1992) The Odor of the Other: Olfactory Symbolism and Cultural Categories. *Ethos* 20(2), 133–166.

Classen, Constance (1999) Other Ways to Wisdom: Learning through the Senses across Cultures. *International Review of Education* 45(3), 269–280.

Cockayne, Emily (2007) *Hubbub*: *Filth, Noise & Stench in England 1600–1770*. New Haven, CT: Yale.

Coen, Deborah (2013) *The Earthquake Observers*: *Disaster Science from Lisbon to Richter*. Chicago, IL: University of Chicago.

Cohen, Jeffrey Jerome, and Lowell Duckert (2015) Introduction. In Jeffrey Jerome Cohen and Lowell Duckert, eds., *Elemental Ecocriticism*: *Thinking with Earth, Air, Water, and Fire*, pp.1–26. Minneapolis, MN: University of Minnesota Press.

Cohen, Jeffrey Jerome (2015) *Stone*: *An Ecology of the Inhuman*. Minneapolis, MN: University of Minnesota.

Cohen, Lara Langer (2022) *Going Underground*: *Race, Space, and the Subterranean in the Nineteenth- Century United States*. Durham, NC: Duke.

Colbatch, John, and Francis Tuthill (1689) *The Doctrine of Acids in the Cure of Diseases Farther Asserted*. London: Brown.

Conty, Arianne (2023) *Grounding God*: *Religious Responses to the Anthropocene*. Albany, NY: SUNY.

Corbin, Alain (1986) *The Foul and the Fragrant*: *Odor and the French Social Imagination*. Cambridge, MA: Harvard.

Cotta, John (1625) *The Infallible True and Assured Witch*. London: Legat.

Crary, Jonathan (1990) *Techniques of the Observer*: *On Vision and Modernity in the Nineteenth Century*. Cambridge, MA: Harvard.

Crawford, Jason (2017) *Allegory and Enchantment*: *An Early Modern Poetics*. Oxford: Oxford.

Crockett, Clayton (2022) *Energy and Change*: *A New Materialist Cosmotheology*. New York: Columbia.

Croll, Oswald Henry Pinnell, and Paracelsus (1657) *Philosophy Reformed & Improved in Four Profound Tractates*. London: M. S. for Lodowick Lloyd.

Cunha, Daniel (2019) The Frontier of Hell: Sicily, Sulfur, and the Rise of the British Chemical Industry, 1750–1840. *Critical Historical Studies* 6(2), 279–302.

Curran, Daniel (1993) *Dead Laws for Dead Men*: *The Politics of Federal Coal Mine Health and Safety Legislation*. Pittsburgh, PA: Pittsburgh.

Daggett, Cara (2019) *The Birth of Energy*: *Fossil Fuels, Thermodynamics, and the Politics of Work*. Durham, NC: Duke.

Daneau, Lambert (1575) *A Dialogue of Witches*. London: East for Watkins.

Darr, Orna (2011) *Marks of an Absolute Witch*: *Evidentiary Dilemmas in Early Modern England*. London: Ashgate.

Das, Nandini, and Nick Davis (2016) Introduction. In Nandini Das and Nick Davis, eds., *Enchantment and Dis- enchantment in Shakespeare and Early Modern Drama: Wonder, the Sacred, and the Supernatural*, pp. 1–17. New York: Routledge.

Debeir, Jean-Claudem Jean-Paul Deléage, and Daniel Hémery (1990) *In the Servitude of Power*: *Energy and Civilization through the Ages*, trans. John Barzman, London: Zed.

DeLay, Tad (2024) *Future of Denial*: *The Ideologies of Climate Change*. London: Verso.

Della Dora, Veronica (2021) *The Mantle of the Earth*: *Genealogies of a Geographical Metaphor*. Chicago, IL: University of Chicago.

DeLoughrey, Elizabeth (2019) *Allegories of the Anthropocene*. Durham, NC: Duke.

Derickson, Alan (2014) *Black Lung*: *Anatomy of a Public Health Disaster*. Ithaca, NY: Cornell.

Derrida, Jacques (2011) *Voice and Phenomenon*: *Introduction to the Problem of the Sign in Husserl's Phenomenology*. Evanston, IL: Northwestern.

Di Cesare, Donatella (2021) *Immunodemocracy*: *Capitalist Asphyxia*. Cambridge, MA: MIT.

De Landa, Manual (2000) *A Thousand Years of Non-Linear History*. New York: Swerve.

Dietrich, Christopher (2017) *Oil Revolution*: *Anticolonial Elites, Sovereign Rights, and the Economic Culture of Decolonization*. Cambridge: Cambridge.

Doganova, Liliana (2024) *Discounting the Future*: *The Ascendancy of a Political Technology*. Princeton, NJ: Zone.

Douglas, Mary (1966) *Purity and Danger; an Analysis of Concepts of Pollution and Taboo*. New York: Praeger.

Douwe, Klaes (2010) *Clean Coal*. New York: Nova Science.

Duckert, Lowell (2015) Earth's Prospects. In Duckert and Lowell, eds., *Elemental Ecocriticism*: *Thinking with Earth, Air, Water, and Fire*, pp. 237–268. Minneapolis, MN: University of Minnesota.

Dugan, Holly (2011) *The Ephemeral History of Perfume*: *Scent and Sense in Early Modern England*. Baltimore, MD: Johns Hopkins.

Eagleton, Terry (1990) *The Ideology of the Aesthetic*. Malden, MA: Blackwell.

Engelmann, Lukas, and Christos Lynteris (2020) *Sulphuric Utopias*: *A History of Maritime Fumigation*. London: MIT.

Engelmann, Sasha (2020) *Sensing Art in the Atmosphere*: *Elemental Lures and Aerosolar Practices*. London: Taylor & Francis.

Evans, Suzanne (2002) The Scent of a Martyr. *Numen* 49(2), 193–211.

Evelyn, John (1661) *Fumifugium, or, The Inconveniencie of the Aer and Smoak of London Dissipated*: *Together with Some Remedies Humbly Proposed*. London: Godbid.

Farrier, David (2019) *Anthropocene Poetics*: *Deep Time, Sacrifice Zones, and Extinction*. Minneapolis, MN: University of Minnesota.

Felli, Romain (2021) *The Great Adaptation*: *Climate, Capitalism and Catastrophe*. London: Verso.

Ferrara, Vincenzo (2015) The Sulphur Mining Industry in Sicily. In Francesco Sorge and Giuseppe Genchi, eds., *Essays on the History of Mechanical Engineering* 31, pp. 111–130. Cham: Springer.

Floyd-Wilson, Mary (2013) *Occult Knowledge, Science, and Gender on the Shakespearean Stage*. Cambridge: Cambridge.

Fors, Hjalmar (2015) *The Limits of Matter*: *Chemistry, Mining, and Enlightenment*. Chicago, IL: University of Chicago.

Foyster, Elizabeth (2010) Sensory Experiences; Smells, Sounds, and Touch. In Elizabeth Foyster and Christopher Whatley, eds., *A History of Everyday Life in Scotland 1600 to* 1800, pp. 217–233. Edinburgh: Edinburgh.

Francis, R. M., and Sebastian Groes (2021) The Making of the Black Country. In R.M. Francis and Sebastian Groes, eds., *Smell, Memory, and Literature in the Black Country*, pp. 1–24. Cham: Palgrave.

Frase, Peter (2016) *Four Futures*: *Life after Capitalism*. London: Verso.

Freese, Barbara (2016) *Coal*: *A Human History*. New York: Basic.

Frehner, Brian (2011) *Finding Oil*: *The Nature of Petroleum Geology, 1859–1920*. Lincoln, NE: Nebraska.

Fressoz, Jean-Baptiste (2024) *Happy Apocalypse*: *A History of Technological Risk*. London: Verso.

Fressoz, Jean-Baptiste, and Fabien Locher (2024) *Chaos in the Heavens*: *The Forgotten History of Climate Change*. London: Verso.

Friedman, Emily (2016) *Reading Smell in Eighteenth-Century Fiction*. Lewisburg, PA: Bucknell.

Gabrys, Jennifer (2016) *Program Earth*: *Environmental Sensing Technology and the Making of a Computational Planet*. Minneapolis, MN: University of Minnesota.

Gabrys, Jennifer (2022) *Citizens of Worlds*: *Open-Air Toolkits for Environmental Struggle*. Minneapolis, MN: University of Minnesota Press.

Gardiner, Beth (2019) *Choked*: *Life and Breath in the Age of Air Pollution*. Chicago, IL: University of Chicago Press, 2019.

Gaskill, Malcolm (2005) *Witchfinders*: *A Seventeenth-Century English Tragedy*. Cambridge, MA: Harvard.

Gasser, Erika (2019) *Vexed with Devils*: *Manhood and Witchcraft in Old and New England*. New York: NYU.

Gaudio, Michael (2008) *Engraving the Savage*: *The New World and Techniques of Civilization*. Minneapolis, MN: University of Minnesota.

Ghosh, Amitav (2017) *The Great Derangement*: *Climate Change and the Unthinkable*. Chicago, IL: University of Chicago.

Glanvill, Joseph, Henry More, and Anthony Horneck (1681) *Saducismus Triumphatus*. London: Collins and Lownds.

Glass, Richard (2016) *Sulfur's Role in the Modern World*. Dordrecht: Springer.

Gobineau, Arthur de (1915) *The Inequality of Human Races*. London: G.P. Putnam's Sons.

Gomez, Rocio (2020) *Silver Veins, Dusty Lungs*: *Mining, Water, and Public Health in Zacatecas, 1835– 1946*. Lincoln, NE: University of Nebraska.

Gómez-Barris, Macarena (2017) *The Extractive Zone*: *Social Ecologies and Decolonial Perspectives*. Durham, NC: Duke.

Goodrick-Clarke, Nicholas (2008) *The Western Esoteric Traditions*: *A Historical Introduction*. Oxford: Oxford.

Goody, Jack (2012) *Metals, Culture and Capitalism*: *An Essay on the Origins of the Modern World*. Cambridge: Cambridge.

Greenblatt, Stephen (2002) *Hamlet in Purgatory*. Princeton, NJ: Princeton.

Griffero, Tonino (2016) *Atmospheres*: *Aesthetics of Emotional Spaces*. London: Taylor & Francis.

Gross Stephen, and Andrew Needham (2023) Towards a New Energy History. In Andrew Needham and Stephen Gross, eds., *New Energies*: *A History of Energy Transitions in Europe and North America*, pp. 3–31. Pittsburgh, PA: Pittsburgh.

Guenther, Genevieve (2024) *The Language of Climate Politics*: *Fossil-Fuel Propaganda and How to Fight It*. Oxford: Oxford.

H. F. (1645) *A True and Exact Relation of the Severall Informations, Examinations, and Confessions of the Late Witches*. London: M.S.

Hales, John (1673) *Golden Remains, of the Ever Memorable, Mr. John Hales*. London: Newcomb.

Haltinner, Kristin, and Dilshani Sarathchandra (2023) *Inside the World of Climate Change Skeptics*. Seattle, WA: University of Washington.

Haraway, Donna (2016) *Staying with the Trouble*: *Making Kin in the Chthulucene*. Durham, NC: Duke.

Harris, Jonathan Gil (2009) *Untimely Matter in the Time of Shakespeare*. Philadelphia, PA: University of Pennsylvania.

Harrison, Mark (1996) "The Tender Frame of Man:" Disease, Climate, and Racial Difference in India and the West Indies. *Bulletin of the History of Medicine* 70, 68–93.

Harte, Jeremy (2023) *Cloven Country*: *The Devil and the English Landscape*. London: Reaktion.

Hasse, Jürgen (2014) Atmospheres as Expression of Medial Power. *Lebenswelt*: *Aesthetics and Philosophy of Experience* 4, 214–229.

Hawhee, Debra (2023) *A Sense of Urgency*: *How the Climate Crisis Is Changing Rhetoric*. Chicago, IL: University of Chicago.

Haynes, Williams (1959) *Brimstone the Stone that Burns*: *The Story of the Frasch Sulphur Industry*. New York: Van Nostrand.

Heine, Stefani (2021) *Poetics of Breathing*: *Modern Literature's Syncope*. Albany, NY: SUNY.

Henckel, Johann Friedrich (1757) *Pyritologia*: *or, A History of the Pyrites, the Principal Body of the Mineral Kingdom*. London: Millar.

Herbert, Thomas (1634) *A Relation of Some Yeares Travaile Begunne Anno 1626*. London: P. William Stansby and Jacob Bloome.

Hiltner, Ken (2007) "Belch's Fire and Rowling Smoke": Air Pollution in *Paradise Lost*. In Christophe Tournu, ed., *Milton, Rights and Liberties*, pp. 293–302. Bern: Peter Lang.

Holmberg, Karen (2013) The Sound of Sulfur and the Smell of Lightning. In Jo Day, ed., *Making Senses of the Past: Toward a Sensory Archaeology*, pp. 49–68. Carbondale, IL: Southern Illinois.

Homza, Lu Ann (2024) *The Child Witches of Olague*. University Park, PA: Penn State.

Howes, David (1991) *The Varieties of Sensory Experience: A Sourcebook in the Anthropology of the Senses*. Toronto: University of Toronto.

Hsu, Hsuan (2020) *The Smell of Risk: Environmental Disparities and Olfactory Aesthetics*. New York: New York University.

Huber, Matthew (2022) *Climate Change as Class War: Building Socialism on a Warming Planet*. London: Verso.

Hughes, David McDermott (2021) *Who Owns the Wind? Climate Crisis and the Hope of Renewable Energy*. London: Verso.

Hulme, Peter (1986) *Colonial Encounters: Europe and the Native Caribbean, 1492–1797*. London: Methuen.

I. H. (1645) *A True Relation of the Araignment of Eighteene Witches*. London: I.H.

Ingold, Tim (2011) *Being Alive: Essays on Movement, Knowledge and Description*. London: Routledge.

Irigaray, Luce (1999) *The Forgetting of Air in Martin Heidegger*. London: Athlone.

Jenner, Mark (2010) Tasting Lichfield, Touching China: Sir John Floyers' Senses. *The Historical Journal* 53(3), 647–670.

Joas, Hans (2021) *The Power of the Sacred: An Alternative to the Narrative of Disenchantment*, trans. Alex Skinner. New York: Oxford.

Johnson, Bob (2019) *Mineral Rites: An Archaeology of the Fossil Economy*. Baltimore, MD: Johns Hopkins.

Johnson, Sherry (2011) *Climate and Catastrophe in Cuba and the Atlantic World in the Age of Revolution*. Chapel Hill, NC: University of North Carolina.

Johnston, Katherine (2013) The Constitution of Empire: Place and Bodily Health in the Eighteenth Century Atlantic. *Atlantic Studies* 10(4), 443–466.

Johnstone, Nathan (2004) The Protestant Devil: The Experience of Temptation in Early Modern England. *The Journal of British Studies* 43(2), 173–205.

Johnstone, Nathan (2006) *The Devil and Demonism in Early Modern England*. Cambridge: Cambridge.

Jonkman, Jesse (2024) *Underground Politics*: *Gold Mining and State-Making in Colombia*. Philadelphia, PA: University of Pennsylvania.

Josephson-Storm, Jason (2017) *Myth of Disenchantment*: *Magic, Modernity, and the Birth of the Human Sciences*. Chicago, IL: University of Chicago.

Jütte, Robert (2005) *A History of the Senses*: *From Antiquity to Cyberspace*. Cambridge: Polity.

Kananoja, Kalle (2016) Infected by the Devil, Cured by Calundu: African Healers in Eighteenth Century Minas Gerais, Brazil. *Social History of Medicine* 29, 490–511.

Kander, Astrid, Paolo Malanima, and Paul Warde (2017) *Power to the People*: *Energy in Europe over the Last Five Centuries*. Princeton, NJ: Princeton.

Kelly, Jack (2009) *Gunpowder*: *Alchemy, Bombards, and Pyrotechnics*: *The History of the Explosive that Changed the World*. New York: Basic.

Kettler, Andrew (2016) Ravishing Odors of Paradise: Jesuits, Olfaction, and Seventeenth Century North American. *Journal of American Studies* 50(4), 827–852.

Kettler, Andrew (2020) Queer Mineralogy and the Depths of Hell: Sulfuric Skills in Early Modern England, the American Frontier, and British Columbia. *Journal of the Canadian Historical Association / Revue de la Société historique du Canada* 30(1), 115–143.

Kettler, Andrew (2022) The Miasmic Theft of Modernity: Sulfuric Aromata and Early Modern Empires. *Venti* 2(2), www.venti-journal.com/andrew-kettler.

Kettler, Andrew (2024) Dispersing the Devil's Stench: Shifting Perceptions of Sulfuric Miasma in Early Modern English Literatures. *Partial Answers*: *Journal of Literature and the History of Ideas* 22(1), 27–53.

Kiechle, Melanie A. (2017) *Smell Detectives*: *An Olfactory History of Nineteenth-Century Urban America*. Seattle: University of Washington Press.

Kitch, Aaron (2016) Enchanted Materialism in Paracelsus, Hobbes, and *Hamlet*. In Nandini Das and Nick Davis, eds., *Enchantment and Disenchantment in Shakespeare and Early Modern Drama*: *Wonder, the Sacred, and the Supernatural*, pp. 72–87. London: Taylor & Francis.

Klare, Michael (2012) *The Race for What's Left*: *The Global Scramble for the World's Last Resources*. New York: Henry Holt.

Klarer, Mario (1999) Cannibalism and Carnivalesque: Incorporation as Utopia in the Early Image of America. *New Literary History* 30(2), 389–410.

Klein, Naomi (2007) *The Shock Doctrine*: *The Rise of Disaster Capitalism*. New York: Metropolitan.

Koeing, Anne (2019) Magicking Madness: Secret Workings and Public Narratives of Disordered Minds in Late Medieval Germany. In David Collins (ed.) *The Sacred and the Sinister*: *Studies in Medieval Religion and Magic*, pp. 201–230. University Park, PA: Penn State.

Koslofsky, Craig (2021). Offshoring the Invisible World? American Ghosts, Witches, and Demons in the Early Enlightenment. *Critical Research on Religion* 9(2), 1–16.

Kramer, Ronald (2020) *Carbon Criminals, Climate Crimes*. New Brunswick: Rutgers.

Kroonenberg, Salomon Bernard, and Andy Brown (2012) *Why Hell Stinks of Sulfur*: *Mythology and Geology of the Underworld*. London: Reaktion.

Kuhn, John (2024) *Making Pagans*: *Theatrical Practice and Comparative Religion in Early Modern England*. Philadelphia, PA: University of Pennsylvania.

Kupperman, Karen (1984) Fear of Hot Climates in the Anglo-American Colonial Experience. *William and Mary Quarterly* 41(2), 213–240.

Kutney, Gerald (2013) *Sulfur*: *History, Technology, Applications & Industry*. Toronto: ChemTec.

Lander, Jesse (2016) Demonism and Disenchantment in the *First Part of the Contention*. In Nandini Das and Nick Davis, eds., *Enchantment and Disenchantment in Shakespeare and Early Modern Drama*: *Wonder, the Sacred, and the Supernatural*, pp. 18–37. London: Taylor & Francis.

Lane, Kris (2005) Africans and Natives in the Mines of Spanish America. In Matthew Restall, ed., *Beyond Black and Red*: *African-native Relations in Colonial Latin America*, pp. 139–184. Albuquerque, NM: New Mexico

Largier, Niklaus (2022) *Figures of Possibility*: *Aesthetic Experience, Mysticism, and the Play of the Senses*. Stanford, CA: Stanford.

Latour, Bruno (1991) *We Have Never Been Modern*, trans. Catherine Porter. Cambridge, MA: Harvard.

Latour, Bruno (2007) *Reassembling the Social*: *An Introduction to Actor-Network-Theory*. Oxford: Oxford.

Lauer, Matthew (2023) *Sensing Disaster*: *Local Knowledge and Vulnerability in Oceania*. Berkeley, CA: University of California.

Lavoisier, Antoine (2011 [1790]) *Elements of Chemistry*. New York: Dover.

Lawrence, Mathew, and Laurie Laybourn-Langton (2022) *Planet on Fire*: *A Manifesto for the Age of Environmental Breakdown*. London: Verso.

LeCain, Timothy (2017) *The Matter of History*: *How Things Create the Past*. Cambridge: Cambridge.

Lepawsky, Josh, and Max Liboiron (2022) *Discard Studies*: *Wasting, Systems, and Power*. Cambridge, MA: MIT.

Léry, Jean de (1990) *History of a Voyage to the Land of Brazil, Otherwise Called America*: trans. Janet Whatley. Berkeley, CA: University of California.

Levine, Laura (2023) *Afterlives of Endor*: *Witchcraft, Theatricality, and Uncertainty from the "Malleus Maleficarum" to Shakespeare*. Ithaca, NY: Cornell.

Lewis, Ronald (1979) "The Darkest Abode of Man:" Black Miners in the First Southern Coal Field 1780–1865. *The Virginia Magazine of History and Biography* 87(2), 190–202.

Liebler, Naomi Conn (1995) *Shakespeare's Festive Tragedy*: *The Ritual Foundations of Genre*. London: Routledge.

Lockwood, Alan (2014) *Silent Epidemic*: *Coal and the Hidden Threat to Health*. Cambridge, MA: MIT.

Lyotard, Jean-François (2015) *Libidinal Economy*. London: Bloomsbury.

MacDuffie, Allen (2014) *Victorian Literature, Energy, and the Ecological Imagination*. Cambridge: Cambridge.

Mallin, Eric S. (2016) The Charm in Macbeth. In Nandini Das and Nick Davis, eds., *Enchantment and Dis-enchantment in Shakespeare and Early Modern Drama*: *Wonder, the Sacred, and the Supernatural*, pp. 55–71. New York: Routledge.

Malm, Andreas (2016) *Fossil Capital*: *The Rise of Steam Power and the Roots of Global Warming*. London: Verso.

Malm, Andreas, and The Zetkin Collective (2021) *White Skin, Black Fuel*: *On the Danger of Fossil Fascism*. London: Verso.

Manley, Lawrence (1995) *Literature and Culture in Early Modern London*. Cambridge: Cambridge.

Marshall, George (2014) *Don't Even Think about It*: *Why Our Brains Are Wired to Ignore Climate Change*. New York: Bloomsbury.

Marston, Andrea (2024) *Subterranean Matters*: *Cooperative Mining and Resource Nationalism in Plurinational Bolivia*. Durham, NC: Duke.

Martin, Randall (2015) *Shakespeare and Ecology*. Oxford: Oxford.

Martyr D'Anghera, Peter (1912 [1516]) *De Orbe Novo, The Eight Decades of Peter Martyr D'Anghera*, trans. Francis Augustus MacNutt. New York: Putnam's Sons.

Masiello, Francine (2018) *The Senses of Democracy*: *Perception, Politics, and Culture in Latin America*. Austin, TX: University of Texas.

Massumi, Brian (2015) *The Power at the End of the Economy*. Durham, NC: Duke.

Mauss, Marcel (1973) *Sociologie et Anthropologie*. Paris: Presses Universitaires de France.

Maxwell, J. Byers (1902) *A Passion for Gold*: *The Story of a South African Mine*. London: Treherne.

Maysilles, Duncan (2011) *Ducktown Smoke: The Southern Appalachian Story of the Supreme Court's First Air Pollution Case*. Chapel Hill, NC: University of North Carolina.

McKinley, Shepherd (2014) *Stinking Stones and Rocks of Gold: Phosphate, Fertilizer, and Industrialization in Postbellum South Carolina*. Gainesville, FL: University Press of Florida.

McCormack, Derek (2018) *Atmospheric Things: On the Allure of Elemental Envelopment*. Durham, NC: Duke, 2018.

McIvor, Arthur, and Ronald Johnston (2016) *Miners' Lung: A History of Dust Disease in British Coal Mining*. London: Routledge.

Melero, Joaquin Perez (2009) From Alchemy to Science: The Scientific Revolution and Enlightenment in Spanish American Mining and Metallurgy. *Geological Society of America*, Memoir 203, 51–61.

Melosi, Martin (2008) *The Sanitary City: Environmental Services in Urban America from Colonial Times to the Present*. Pittsburgh, PA: Pittsburgh.

Merleau-Ponty, Maurice (1962) *Phenomenology of Perception*. London: Routledge.

Mészáros, István (2010 [1995]) *Beyond Capital: Toward a Theory of Transition*. New York: Monthly Review.

Meyer, Beat (1977) *Sulfur, Energy, and Environment*. Amsterdam: Elsevier.

Meziane, Mohamed Amer (2024) *The States of the Earth: An Ecological and Racial History of Secularization*. London: Verso.

Mignolo, Walter (2011) *The Darker Side of Western Modernity: Global Futures, Decolonial Options*. Durham, NC: Duke.

Miller, Elizabeth Carolyn (2021) *Extraction Ecologies and the Literature of the Long Exhaustion*. Princeton, NJ: Princeton.

Mitchell, Timothy (2013) *Carbon Democracy: Political Power in the Age of Oil*. London: Verso.

Montaigne, Michel de (1700) *Essays of Michael, Seigneur de Montaigne*. London: Gillyflower, Hensman, Wellington, and Hindmarsh.

Monteon, Michael (2019) John T. North, the Nitrate King, and Chile's Lost Future. In Raymond Dumett, ed., *Mining Tycoons in the Age of Empire, 1870–1945: Entrepreneurship, High Finance, Politics and Territorial Expansion*, pp. 109–126. Farnham: Ashgate.

Montrie, Chad (2003) *To Save the Land and People: A History of Opposition to Surface Coal Mining in Appalachia*. Chapel Hill, NC: University of North Carolina.

Moore, Jason (2015) *Capitalism in the Web of Life: Ecology and the Accumulation of Capital*. London: Verso.

Morgan, Jennifer (2004) *Laboring Women: Reproduction and Gender in New World Slavery.* Philadelphia, PA: University of Pennsylvania.

Morrison, Susan Signe (2015) *The Literature of Waste: Material Ecopoetics and Ethical Matter.* New York: Palgrave Macmillan.

Morton, Michael Quentin (2017) *Empires and Anarchies: A History of Oil in the Middle East.* London: Reaktion.

Morton, Timothy (2014) *Hyperobjects: Philosophy and Ecology after the End of the World.* Minneapolis, MN: University of Minnesota.

Morton, Timothy (2019) *Being Ecological.* Cambridge, MA: MIT.

Mosley, Stephen (2001) *The Chimney of the World: A History of Smoke Pollution in Victorian and Edwardian Manchester.* Cambridge: Cambridge.

Mudahar, Mohinder (2013) *Fertilizer, Sulfur, and Food Production.* Dordrecht: Springer.

Müller, Simone (2023) *The Toxic Ship: The Voyage of the Khian Sea and the Global Waste Trade.* Seattle, WA: University of Washington.

Mulry, Kate Luce (2021) *An Empire Transformed: Remolding Bodies and Landscapes in the Restoration Atlantic.* New York: New York University.

Mundy, Barbara (2021) No Longer Home: The Smellscape of Mexico City, 1500–1600. *Ethnohistory* 68 (1), 77–101.

Murray, Lisa (2017) "Big Smoke Stacks": Competing Memories of the Sounds and Smells of Industrial Heritage. In Joy Damousi and Paula Hamilton, eds., *A Cultural History of Sound, Memory and the Senses*, pp.179–193. New York: Routledge.

Myers, Kathleen Ann (2010) *Fernández de Oviedo's Chronicle of America: A New History for a New World*, translations by Nina M. Scott. Austin, TX: University of Texas.

Nash, June (1993) *We Eat the Mines and the Mines Eat Us: Dependency and Exploitation in Bolivian Tin Mines.* New York: Columbia.

Neiman, Susan (2015) *Evil in Modern Thought: An Alternative History of Philosophy.* Princeton, NJ: Princeton.

Newhauser, Richard (2016) The Multisensoriality of Place and the Chaucerian Multisensual. In Annette Kern-Stähler, Beatrix Busse, and Wietse de Boer, eds., *The Five Senses in Medieval and Early Modern England*, pp. 199–218. Leiden: Brill.

Newman, William (2019) *Newton the Alchemist: Science, Enigma, and the Quest for Nature's "Secret Fire."* Princeton, NJ: Princeton.

Nikiforuk, Andrew (2012) *The Energy of Slaves: Oil and the New Servitude.* Berkeley, CA: Greystone.

Nixon, Rob (2011) *Slow Violence and the Environmentalism of the Poor.* Cambridge, MA: Harvard.

Ogawa, Tadashi (2021) *Phenomenology of Wind and Atmosphere*. Milan: Mimesis International.

Olivarius, Kathryn (2022) *Necropolis*: *Disease, Power, and Capitalism in the Cotton Kingdom*. Cambridge, MA: Harvard.

Oppenheimer, Clive (2023) *Mountains of Fire*: *The Secret Lives of Volcanoes*. London: Hodder & Stoughton.

Orr, David (2004) *Earth in Mind*: *On Education, Environment, and the Human Prospect*. Washington, DC: Island.

Ossa-Richardson, Anthony (2013) *The Devil's Tabernacle*: *The Pagan Oracles in Early Modern Thought*. Princeton, NJ: Princeton.

Otter, Chris (2008) *The Victorian Eye*: *A Political History of Light and Vision in Britain, 1800–1910*. Chicago, IL: University of Chicago.

Paliewicz, Nicholas (2024) *Extraction Politics*: *Rio Tinto and the Corporate Persona*. University Park, PA: Penn State.

Panagia, Davide (2010) *Political Life of Sensation*. Durham, NC: Duke.

Parenti, Christian (2012) *Tropic of Chaos*: *Climate Change and the New Geography of Violence*. New York: Nation.

Parr, Joy (2010) *Sensing Changes*: *Technologies, Environments, and the Everyday, 1953–2003*. Vancouver: UBC.

Pearson, Thomas (2017) *When the Hills Are Gone*: *Frac Sand Mining and the Struggle for Community*. Minneapolis, MN: University of Minnesota.

Pennartz, Cyriel (2024) *The Consciousness Network*: *How the Brain Creates Our Reality*. London: Taylor & Francis.

Perkins, William (1610) *A Discourse of the Damned Art of Witchcraft*. Cambridge: Legge.

Perras, Jean-Alexandre, and Erika Wicky (2021) Olfactive Culture and Mediality of Smells. In Jean-Alexandre Perra and Erika Wicky, eds., *Mediality of Smells*, pp. 15–28. Oxford: Peter Lang.

Pettman, Dominic (2017) *Sonic Intimacy*: *Voice, Species, Technics (or, How To Listen to the World)*. Stanford, CA: Stanford.

Pickett, Holly Crawford (2011) The Idolatrous Nose: Incense on the Early Modern Stage. In Jane Hwang Degenhardt and Elizabeth Williamson, eds., *Religion and Drama in Early Modern England*: *The Performance of Religion on the Renaissance Stage*, pp. 19–38. Farnham: Ashgate.

Plattes, Gabriel (1679) *A Discovery of Subterranean Treasure*. London: Parker.

Pluymers, Keith (2016) Atlantic Iron: Wood Scarcity and the Political Ecology of Early English Expansion. *William and Mary Quarterly* 73(3), 389–426.

Pomeranz, Kenneth (2000) *The Great Divergence*: *China, Europe, and the Making of the Modern World Economy*. Princeton, NJ: Princeton.

Prager, Ellen (2020) *Dangerous Earth*: *What We Wish We Knew about Volcanoes, Hurricanes, Climate Change, Earthquakes, and More*. Chicago, IL: University of Chicago.

Pratt, Mary Louise (2022) *Planetary Longings*. Durham, NC: Duke.

Preedy, Chloe Kathleen (2022) *Aerial Environments on the Early Modern Stage*: *Theatres of the Air, 1576–1609*. Oxford: Oxford.

Pudney, Eric (2019) *Scepticism and Belief in English Witchcraft Drama, 1538–1681*. Lund: Lund.

Pynsent, R. B. (1993) The Devil's Stench and Living Water: A Study of Demons and Adultery in Czech Vernacular Literature of the Middle Ages and Renaissance. *The Slavonic and East European Review* 71(4), 601-630.

Rancière, Jacques (2004) *The Politics of Aesthetics*: *The Distribution of the Sensible*. London: Bloomsbury.

Read, Richard (2022) *Sensory Perception, History and Geology*: *The Afterlife of Molyneux's Question in British, American and Australian Landscape Painting and Cultural Thought*. Cambridge: Cambridge.

Redden, Andrew (2013) Vipers under the Altar Cloth: Satanic and Angelic Forms in Seventeenth-Century New Granada. In Fernando Cervantes and Andrew Redden, eds., *Angels, Demons and the New World*, pp. 146–170. Cambridge: Cambridge.

Redfield, Marc (2003) *The Politics of Aesthetics*: *Nationalism, Gender, Romanticism*. Stanford, CA: Stanford.

Reinarz, Jonathan (2012) Learning to Use Their Senses: Visitors to Voluntary Hospitals in Eighteenth-Century England. *Journal for Eighteenth-Century Studies* 35(4), 505–520.

Ribas, Andrés Pérez de, and Daniel Reff (1999) *History of the Triumphs of Our Holy Faith Amongst the Most Barbarous and Fierce Peoples of the New World*. Tucson, AZ: University of Arizona.

Robertson, David (2009) Incensed over Incense: Incense and Community in Seventeenth-Century Literature. In Roger D. Sell and Anthony W. Johnson, eds., *Writing and Religion in England, 1558–1689*: *Studies in Community-Making and Cultural Memory*, pp. 389–409. Burlington: Ashgate.

Robins, Nicholas (2011) *Mercury, Mining, and Empire*: *The Human and Ecological Cost of Colonial Silver Mining in the Andes*. Bloomington, IN: Indiana.

Robinson, Katelynn (2019) *The Sense of Smell in the Middle Ages*: *A Source of Certainty*. London: Taylor & Francis.

Rojas, Rochelle (2025) *Bad Christians and Hanging Toads*: *Witch Crafting in Northern Spain, 1525–1675*. Ithaca, NY: Cornell.

Rosen, William (2010) *The Most Powerful Idea in the World: A Story of Steam, Industry, and Invention.* Chicago, IL: University of Chicago.

Rosa, Hartmut (2020) *Resonance: A Sociology of Our Relationship to the World.* Cambridge, UK: Polity.

Rosner, David, and Gerald Markowitz (2002) *Deceit and Denial: The Deadly Politics of Industrial Pollution.* Berkeley, CA: California.

Rothschild, Rachel Emma (2019) *Poisonous Skies: Acid Rain and the Globalization of Pollution.* Chicago, IL: University of Chicago.

Rotter, Andrew (2011) Empires of the Senses: How Seeing, Hearing, Smelling, Tasting, and Touching Shaped Imperial Encounters. *Diplomatic History* 35(1), 3–19.

Saito, Kohei (2024) *Slow Down: The Degrowth Manifesto.* London: Astra.

Salmon, William (1683) *Doron Medicum; or, a Supplement to the New London Dispensatory.* London: Salmon.

Salter, Alan (2010) Early Modern Empiricism and the Discourse of the Senses. In Charles Wolfe and Ofer Ga l, eds., *The Body as Object and Instrument of Knowledge: Embodied Empiricism in Early Modern Science*, pp. 59–74. Dordrecht: Springer.

Saltmarsh, Chris (2021) *Burnt: Fighting for Climate Justice.* London: Pluto.

Santiago, Myrna (2006) *The Ecology of Oil: Environment, Labor, and the Mexican Revolution, 1900–1938.* Cambridge: Cambridge.

Schellenberg, Susanna (2018) *The Unity of Perception: Content, Consciousness, Evidence.* Oxford: Oxford.

Scheyder, Ernest (2024) *The War Below: Lithium, Copper, and the Global Battle to Power Our Lives.* London: Atria.

Schiebinger, Londa (1993) *Nature's Body: Gender in the Making of Modern Science.* Boston, MA: Beacon.

Schwartz, Stuart (2015) *Sea of Storms: A History of Hurricanes in the Greater Caribbean from Columbus to Katrina.* Princeton, NJ: Princeton.

Scot, Reginald (1886 [1584]). *The Discoverie of Witchcraft.* London: Brome.

Seiler, Thomas (1992) Filth and Stench as Aspects of the Iconography of Hell. In Clifford Davidson and Thomas Seiler, eds., *The Iconography of Hell*, pp. 132–140. Kalamazoo, MI: Central Michigan.

Serres, Michel (2009) *The Five Senses: A Philosophy of Mingled Bodies.* London: Continuum.

Seth, Suman (2018) *Difference and Disease: Medicine, Race, and the Eighteenth-Century British Empire.* Cambridge: Cambridge.

Sharpe, Christina (2016) *In the Wake: On Blackness and Being.* Durham, NC: Duke.

Shotwell, Alexis (2011) *Knowing Otherwise: Race, Gender, and Implicit Understanding*. University Park, PA: Pennsylvania State.

Silkenat, David (2022) *Scars on the Land: An Environmental History of Slavery in the American South*. New York: Oxford.

Slack, Charles (2002) *Noble Obsession: Charles Goodyear, Thomas Hancock, and the Race to Unlock the Greatest Industrial Secret of the 19th Century*. New York: Hyperion.

Smil, Vaclav (2016) *Energy Transitions*. Westport, CT: ABC-CLIO.

Smith, Crosbie (2018) *Coal, Steam and Ships: Engineering, Enterprise and Empire on the Nineteenth-Century Seas*. Cambridge: Cambridge.

Soper, Kate (2023) *Post-Growth Living: For an Alternative Hedonism*. London: Verso.

Spears, Ellen Griffith (2014) *Baptized in PCBs: Race, Pollution, and Justice in an All-American Town*. Chapel Hill, NC: University of North Carolina.

Staden, Hans (2008 [1557]) *Hans Staden's True History: An Account of Cannibal Captivity in Brazil*, trans. Neil L. Whitehead and Michael Harbsmeier. Durham, NC: Duke.

Strachey, John (1727) *Observations on the Different Strata of Earths and Minerals: More Parricularly of Such as Are Found in the Coal-Mines of Great Britian*. London: Walthoe.

Steel, Karl (2015) Creeping Things: Spontaneous Generation and Material Creativity. In Jeffrey Jerome Cohen and Lowell Duckert, eds., *Elemental Ecocriticism: Thinking with Earth, Air, Water, and Fire*, pp. 209–236. Minneapolis, MN: University of Minnesota.

Stengers, Isabelle (2015) *In Catastrophic Times: Resisting the Coming Barbarism*. London: Open Humanities.

Stevenson, William (1575) *A Ryght Pithy, Pleasaunt and Merie Comedie: Gammer Gurton's Nedle*. London: Colwell.

Stoler, Ann Laura (1995) *Race and the Education of Desire: Foucault's History of Sexuality and the Colonial Order of Things*. Durham, NC: Duke.

Stoll, Mark (2022) *Profit: An Environmental History*. Cambridge: Polity.

Stradling, David (1999) *Smokestacks and Progressives: Environmentalists, Engineers and Air Quality in America, 1881–1951*. Baltimore, MD: Johns Hopkins.

Studnicki-Gizbert, Daviken, and David Schecter (2010) The Environmental Dynamics of a Colonial Fuel-Rush: Silver Mining and Deforestation in New Spain 1522 to 1810. *Environmental History* 15, 94–119.

Studnicki-Gizbert, Daviken (2022) *The Three Deaths of Cerro de San Pedro: Four Centuries of Extractivism in a Small Mexican Mining Town*. Chapel Hill, NC: University of North Carolina.

Swarbrick, Steven (2023) *The Environmental Unconscious*: *Ecological Poetics from Spenser to Milton*. Minneapolis, MN: University of Minnesota.

Taussig, Michael (1980) *The Devil and Commodity Fetishism in South America*. Chapel Hill, NC: University of North Carolina.

Taussig, Michael (1992) *Mimesis and Alterity*: *A Particular History of the Senses*. New York: Routledge.

Taylor, Diana (2004) Scenes of Cognition: Performance and Conquest. *Theatre Journal* 56(3), 353–372.

Taylor, Diana (2020) *¡Presente! The Politics of Presence*. Durham, NC: Duke.

Taylor, Jesse Oak (2016) *The Sky of Our Manufacture*: *The London Fog in British Fiction from Dickens to Woolf*. Charlottesville, VA: University of Virginia.

Testot, Laurent (2020) *Cataclysms*: *An Environmental History of Humanity*. Chicago, IL: University of Chicago.

Thébaud-Sorger Marie (2018) Capturing the Invisible: Heat, Steam and Gases in France and Great Britain, 1750–1800. In Lissa Roberts and Simon Werrett, eds., *Compound Histories*: *Materials, Governance, and Production, 1760–1840*, pp. 85–105. Amsterdam: Brill.

Theile, Verene (2016) Demonising Macbeth. In Lisa Hopkins and Helen Ostovich, eds., *Magical Transformations on the Early Modern English Stage*, pp. 75–90. New York: Taylor & Francis.

Thomas, Keith (1971) *Religion and the Decline of Magic*. New York: Penguin.

Thomson, Jennifer (2019) *The Wild and the Toxic*: *American Environmentalism and the Politics of Health*. Chapel Hill, NC: University of North Carolina

Thorsheim, Peter (2006) *Inventing Pollution*: *Coal, Smoke, and Culture in Britain Since 1800*. Athens, OH: Ohio.

Toadvine, Ted (2024) *The Memory of the World*: *Deep Time, Animality, and Eschatology*. Minneapolis, MN: University of Minnesota.

Toelle, Jutta (2017) Mission Soundscapes: Demons, Jesuits, and Sounds in Antonio Ruiz de Montoya's *Conquista Espiritual* (1639). In Daniela Hacke and Paul Musselwhite, eds., *Empire of the Senses*: *Sensory Practices of Colonialism in Early America*, pp. 67–87. Leiden: Brill.

Tremblay, Jean-Thomas (2022) *Breathing Aesthetics*. Durham, NC: Duke.

Trigg, Dylan (2021) Introduction. In Dylan Trigg, ed., *Atmospheres and Shared Emotions*, pp 1–14. London: Taylor & Francis.

Tryon, Thomas (1682) *A Treatise of Cleanness in Meats, and Drinks, of the Preparation of Food*. London: Curtis.

Tsing, Anna Lowenhaupt (2017) *The Mushroom at the End of the World*: *On the Possibility of Life in Capitalist Ruins*. Princeton, NJ: Princeton.

Tuan, Yi- Fu (1974) *Topophilia: A Study of Environmental Perception, Attitudes, and Values*. Englewood Cliffs, NJ: Prentice Hall.

Turner, Alice (1993) *The History of Hell*. New York: Harcourt Brace.

Turner, James Morton (2022). *Charged: A History of Batteries and Lessons for a Clean Energy Future*. Seattle, WA: University of Washington.

Usher, Phillip John (2019) *Exterranean: Extraction in the Humanist Anthropocene*. New York: Fordham.

Valenčius, Conevery Bolton (2004) *The Health of the Country: How American Settlers Understood Themselves and Their Land*. New York: Basic.

Vergara, Germán (2021) *Fueling Mexico: Energy and Environment, 1850–1950*. Cambridge: Cambridge.

Viveiros de Castro, Eduardo (2015) *Cannibal Metaphysics*. Minneapolis, MN: University of Minnesota.

Von Hippel, Frank (2020) *The Chemical Age: How Chemists Fought Famine and Disease, Killed Millions, and Changed Our Relationship with the Earth*. Chicago, IL: University of Chicago.

Von Mossner, Alexa Weik (2017) *Affective Ecologies: Empathy, Emotion, and Environmental Narrative*. Columbus, OH: Ohio State.

Voyles, Traci Brynne (2015) *Wastelanding: Legacies of Uranium Mining in Navajo Country*. Minneapolis, MN: University of Minnesota.

Wafer, Lionel, and George Parker Winship (1903) *A New Voyage and Description of the Isthmus of America*. Cleveland, OH: Burrows.

Wagner, Gernot, and Martin Weitzman (2015) *Climate Shock: The Economic Consequences of a Hotter Planet*. Princeton, NJ: Princeton.

Wainwright, Joel, and Geoff Mann (2018) *Climate Leviathan: A Political Theory of Our Planetary Future*. London: Verso.

Waldron, Jennifer Elizabeth (2013) *Reformations of the Body: Idolatry, Sacrifice, and Early Modern Theater*. New York: Springer.

Walker, Brett (2011). *Toxic Archipelago: A History of Industrial Disease in Japan*. Seattle, WA: University of Washington.

Wallace-Wells, David (2019) *The Uninhabitable Earth: Life After Warming*. London: Crown.

Walsham, Alexandra (2008) The Reformation and "The Disenchantment of the World" Reassessed. *Historical Journal* 51(2), 497–528.

Wark, McKenzie (2015) *Molecular Red: Theory for the Anthropocene*. London: Verso.

Watson, Andrew (2016) Coal in Canada. In Ruth W. Sandwell, ed., *Powering Up Canada: A History of Power, Fuel, and Energy from 1600*, pp. 213–250. Montreal: McGill-Queen's.

Watson, Thomas (1671) *The Beatitudes, or, A Discourse upon Part of Christs Famous Sermon on the Mount.* London: Smith.

Weekly Memorials for the Ingenious; or, an Account of Books Lately Set Forth in Several Languages. With Other Accounts Relating to Arts and Sciences. No. 1-50. (1682) London: Faithorne and Kersey.

Weemes, John (1636) *A Treatise of the Foure Degenerate Sonnes.* London: Cotes.

Wentworth Smith, and William Shakespeare (1709). *The Puritan: or the Widow of Watling-Street [By W.S., I.E. Wentworth Smith? Sometimes Attributed to William Shakespeare. With an Engraved Frontispiece.* London: N. Pub.

Whitehead, Mark (2011) *State, Science and the Skies*: *Governmentalities of the British Atmosphere.* Hoboken, NJ: Wiley.

Widener, Patricia (2021) *Toxic and Intoxicating Oil*: *Discovery, Resistance, and Justice in Aotearoa, New Zealand.* New Brunswick, NJ: Rutgers.

Williams, Edgar (2021) *Breathing: An Inspired History.* London: Reaktion.

Williams, Raymond (1975) *The Country and the City.* Oxford: Oxford.

Wrigley, Edward (2010) *Energy and the English Industrial Revolution.* Cambridge: Cambridge.

Wrigley, E. A. (2016) *The Path to Sustained Growth*: *England's Transition from an Organic Economy to an Industrial Revolution.* Cambridge: Cambridge.

Wynn, Graeme (2007) *Canada and Arctic North America*: *An Environmental History.* Santa Barbara, CA: ABC-CLIO.

Yusoff, Kathryn (2018) *A Billion Black Anthropocenes or None.* Minneapolis, MN: University of Minnesota.

Zallen, Jeremy (2019) *American Lucifers*: *The Dark History of Artificial Light, 1750–1865.* Chapel Hill, NC: University of North Carolina.

Printed by Integrated Books International,
United States of America